LAUGHING ALL OVER THE WORLD

MY LIFE MARRIED TO STATUS QUO

Laughing All Over the World

MY LIFE MARRIED TO STATUS QUO

PATTY PARFITT
with Mandy Bruce

BLAKE

Published by Blake Publishing Ltd,
3 Bramber Court, 2 Bramber Road,
London W14 9PB, England

First published in paperback in Great Britain 1998

ISBN 1 85782 198X

All rights reserved. No part of this publication may be reproduced, stored in a retrieval system, or in any form or by any means, without the prior permission in writing of the publisher, nor be otherwise circulated in any form of binding or cover other than that in which it is published and without a similar condition including this condition being imposed on the subsequent purchaser.

British Library Cataloguing-in-Publication Data:
A catalogue record for this book is available
from the British Library.

Typeset by BCP

Printed in Great Britain by
Creative Print and Design (Wales), Ebbw Vale, Gwent

1 3 5 7 9 10 8 6 4 2

© Text copyright Patty Parfitt/Mandy Bruce 1998

Cover and inside lettering by Ralph Steadman for Save the Children

It should also be acknowledged that
Status Quo: The Authorised Biography by John Shearlaw proved an invaluable tool in researching this book.

This book is dedicated to the
memory of all the good, fun years.
And to our number one fan,
Harry, with love.

Acknowledgements

I would like to thank all the people who have helped me with this book — and who have supported me during these last few difficult years. Especially Ron and Claire Brown, Alan and Dayle Lancaster, Stephanie Pine. Cousins Sue and Ben, my mother, Daisy, and late father, Stan, my brother Stanley and sister Marion and their children, Lindsay, Brenda, Marcela, Paula, Raka and Gemma from Pre-Prep. Also the teachers at Milbourne Junior for helping Harry through a difficult time, to Wendy, Jenny and Hen, Jennifer and Silvia and the wonderful Feltonfleet school. All at Blake Publishing, John Blake for the first interview all those years ago — now he's got the book! — and Mandy Bruce who adapted my words from years of diaries and mountains of notes.

But not least of all thanks to my Harry, my reason for survival, for giving me reasons to carry on — instead of ending up in a loony bin!

Thanks, too, to Karen W. for remaining cheerful and enthusiastic through all that word processing. Love and thanks to Peago for the paper, points, etc. Also to Sue D., Marisa H. and Ross T. for their continued support.

Contents

Acknowledgements		vii
Chapter One	Picture of a Matchstick Man	1
Chapter Two	So Ends Another Life	17
Chapter Three	You're Just What I Was Looking For Today	35
Chapter Four	Down, Down, Deeper and Down Under	67
Chapter Five	Something About You Baby I Like	81
Chapter Six	Ain't Complaining	93
Chapter Seven	Lonely Nights	101
Chapter Eight	So Ends Another Life	107
Chapter Nine	Run to Mummy	117
Chapter Ten	Rockin' All Over the World	131
Chapter Eleven	Going Downtown Tonight	149
Chapter Twelve	What You're Proposing	169
Chapter Thirteen	Fun, Fun, Fun	187
Chapter Fourteen	Down the Dustpipe	209
Chapter Fifteen	A Mess of the Blues	233
Epilogue		257

1

Picture of a Matchstick Man

The river Thames is deceptive. On sunny days it welcomes you to play about in boats, or walk along its banks from the country to The City, but underneath the current is dangerously fast and strong and the water often treacherously cold. Lean over a London bridge, peer down and its grey muddy ripples are hypnotic, inviting you to jump. About two hundred people accept the invitation every year. Half of them are lucky — the current carries them straight to the riverbank. But, as for the rest, the shock incapacitates them, and the Thames soon swallows them up; an ebbing spring tide of four knots moves faster than any human can walk and it's impossible to fight it. The tide carries them off to deposit their bodies, far downstream, in Wapping or Tilbury or even beyond.

To my Ricky it seemed as good a way to go as any. He wasn't rockin' all over the world any more — Status Quo were finished with the road, had played their last tour, and their last

Patty Parfitt

concert. In fact he wasn't rockin' very much at all — just down to The Raven pub a few yards from the Battersea flat in Valiant House, the flat was a nice enough two-bedroomed place but you could hardly compare it to the luxury five star hotels he was used to. The money situation didn't bear thinking about.

He owed the taxman half a million and couldn't pay the bills. Being a rock megastar — but broke — in the booming London of the late Eighties was no fun, especially when everyone around him was loaded, planning their next holiday in Mustique on the car phone while driving their Porsches to the next trendy watering hole.

Miserable to be broke, especially when the phone wasn't ringing much, he'd lost his licence for the third time and was reduced to being chauffeured around by me, his girlfriend, in my dad's borrowed car — and an Allegro at that. Especially when the champagne had to come courtesy of Peter Stringfellow or anyone else he could blag a bottle from.

Rick's divorce from Marietta had been expensive and painful. A cash fuck-up meant the *End of the Road* tour didn't bring in the readies it should have and Rick was down to £100 a week hand-out from his accountant. What a way to treat a rock star — so he doesn't even know where his next gramme of coke is coming from!

But it wasn't the coke — or the whisky — that made him lean further and further over the bridge. It was the devil. The devil was back in his head, taunting him, telling him things, telling him what to do. He hated to listen but he couldn't help it. The devil was telling him it was all finished. The devil was telling him he was no good. The devil was telling him that he was a bad person and that everyone hated him. It was better to jump ... go on, jump ...

Back in Valiant House I was nursing the bruises around my neck where he'd tried to strangle me. And I was tearing my hair out with worry.

Laughing All Over The World

Poor Rick. He was in a bad way. It was a bad time. I forget what sparked it off. I think Marietta was asking for more money. Or maybe it was that Francis Rossi was up to his old tricks and being a bastard again, putting Rick down, pushing him aside. The Sly Fox, that's what Rick has always called him. Rick hates not having any money, and he hates not having a car. Everyone else seemed to have loads of money at the time. He had a bad case of what he'd call the NIPS — the Never-Ending Inebriated Parfitt Syndrome. And on top of everything he was sticking far too much Niki up his nose. That's what he used to call coke — Niki Lauder, after the racing driver. Niki Lauder — powder — fast!

But it had been a normal sort of day, a normal sort of week. Perhaps not everyone's idea of normal but a Parfitt/Quo normal day.

Usually we'd wake up at about ten and get a cup of tea. Then we'd go back to bed for another couple of hours for what Rick called his Second Kip. He always loved his Second Kip, that was his favourite one. So we'd go back to bed to sleep — nothing else, just sleep. He isn't a randy morning man.

Then it was up and dressed and down to The Raven, the oldest pub in Battersea, all red-flocked wallpaper and worn carpet to match, a grotty place but with a nice atmosphere, and Rick was popular with the lads down there. Some of them were a pain in the arse but all of them liked to be able to introduce Rick as their friend and Rick enjoyed that too.

So he'd go down there and graciously accept a few pints then move on to vodka, or whatever else was on offer, and we'd have a spot of lunch and come home to watch the telly.

Rick watches telly morning, noon and night. He'll watch anything but he loves sport: athletics, football, wrestling — especially Sumo wrestling. He'd watch soaps and children's programmes. Whatever was on he'd watch and, if it was sport, so much the better.

Patty Parfitt

I used to sit and watch telly with him. Usually I'd try and do some housework but Rick didn't like it. 'Sit down,' he'd say. 'I don't like you doing that — I want you here with me.' I had to think up an excuse to do the housework so I'd say I was going to the loo.

'You've been a long time in the loo,' he'd say. In fact, I'd sneaked into the kitchen and done the ironing, emptied the rubbish or put the washing on! Rick hates to be alone. He needs you there — all the time and he needs to touch you to know that you're there. In the car, he has to have a hand on your arm or your leg. He's like a baby. It was weird, strange. I've never met anyone so insecure.

So we'd sit and watch telly, or I'd go shopping for food in my Dad's Allegro, if I could borrow it. After all his Porsches and Bentleys, Rick could hardly bring himself to call it a car. Sometimes we'd go clothes shopping. Rick loves shopping.

'Right,' he'd say, 'we've got the food, now let's go and buy something, let's go and buy me a jacket.' And off we'd go to spend more money we didn't have.

Then it was back to get ready to go out. First, Rick would choose his outfit. There was a lot to choose from. He'd open the wardrobe and a look of intense concentration crossed his face — the Valentino suit? Or the leather trousers? Appearances were very important.

Then he'd turn his attention to me. He had to pick everything from the colour of the nail varnish I wore to my hairstyle. He'd choose my jewellery and if he didn't like the colour lipstick I had on, then it had to go. He told me which dress to wear and even chose my underwear.

He'd say, 'Wear the black bra. Now — what colour knickers have you got on?'

'Black ones.'

'No, wear white knickers.'

Rick adores white underwear.

Sometimes I rebelled and disappeared into the bedroom

alone. When I came back he'd say, 'Did you put the white ones on?'

I'd say, 'Yeah,' but I hadn't. I was still wearing my black knickers or none.

But he always found out — even before we got home. He loves to look up girls' skirts. Of course, he couldn't say anything in front of the people we were out with, but one of his favourite tricks was to knock his packet of cigarettes off the table. Then down he'd go and have a look up my skirt. And then, God help me, he'd see and give me such a dirty look across the table.

Once I was dressed to his satisfaction we'd go off to the pub to have a few drinks. We'd usually leave at six and if Rick said we were leaving at six he meant it. Rick is a time-keeper. He's always punctual and he expects you to be too. It's no good saying you were held up in traffic or got lost. Why didn't you make allowances for delays? There's never any excuse!

After the drinks, it was on to the Italian restaurant where we'd dine on the most expensive food washed down with the most expensive wine. Rick is generous, even when he hasn't got any money. 'Champagne everyone? I'll pay for it.' He loves to impress.

At home it was a different story; always beans on one and egg on one, or 'swimmers in a bag'. Rick loves those frozen fish steaks in parsley sauce, and, of course, a proper roast dinner. He said I made the best roast in the world — even better than his Mum's! He'd say I'd lost it now!

But, out, we had certain standards to keep up. He loves wine lists. In restaurants he grabs one and runs his finger down it. 'Right, here's the wines — and here's the prices. What's that?' he'd say, looking at the price first. Usually it cost a fortune. 'Looks good, let's have that!'

Rick loves that kind of thing and when he's in a hotel he really lets rip. Once, when he'd had a bit to drink, he ordered a £550 bottle of wine. 'I want this fucking wine — go and get it for me!' When the waiter came back with the bottle, Rick

Patty Parfitt

took one swig and passed out!

But I usually enjoyed our meals out. Then we'd leap into a cab and hit a club. Stringfellows or Bootleggers were our usual haunts at the time — besides we always got free champagne at both because Rick was a celebrity and it did the clubs good to have famous people around. Thank heavens!

It was great. Bootleggers was Rick's favourite. It was similar to Stringfellows: lots of weird lights and mirrors, with plenty of girls in skintight outfits. But it was a great atmosphere and Mark Raymond, the owner, became a very good friend. He was really good to Rick, when things were tough, a smashing man. Sadly he died in a car crash.

Mark used to own a couple of shops down the King's Road and, when we were really broke, he used to dress me, too — to Rick's specifications of course.

But one of the greatest attractions of Bootleggers was a bloke who hung out there. He was an actor who'd played bit parts in all sorts of films including *Gandhi* and later he appeared in *EastEnders*.

But it wasn't his acting ability that Rick appreciated — he was the coke supplier for the club. He wasn't a dealer as such, but he knew a man who was, so Rick would just ask him for some coke, he would make the call and the Niki would arrive by cab.

Rick always did a line or two before we went out — just to get in the mood. Then once we got to the club — and our man had come up trumps — Rick would give me some and I'd go to the Ladies with my credit card and he'd go to the Gents with his. The loos in that place got really crowded! Everyone was in there at one time or another during the night — and everyone was doing it! At least that's what Rick said.

I can't say I didn't enjoy the coke — I did. But I never felt like it until I'd had a drink or three. Then once we got to the club it was a trip to the loo and a line every half hour or so for Rick. I didn't do too much — I preferred drinking.

But Rick encouraged me to take coke. 'If you don't do it

with me then I'll go and find someone else who will,' he'd say. So, of course, I did.

Every half an hour or so we'd trot to the loo, sometimes more often if he met people we knew. But soon it began to get ridiculous — and ridiculously expensive. We'd often go through nearly two grammes a night — which was nearly £140 — and, since Rick had only £100 a week, we had to spend my money. I'd just come back from a long stay in Australia and brought £6,000 savings home with me. It was gone in a month! Apart from the Niki, the rock star lifestyle didn't come cheap. I certainly paid my share but even I didn't think it would all disappear so quickly!

I tried to get Rick to cut back a bit but he wasn't having any of it. If I said anything he'd retaliate with something cruel like: 'If you can't stand the pressure you shouldn't be here.' Or we'd have tears. Then it would be: 'Can't you see I'm just doing this because I can't handle anything. I need to get my head straight. I'm trying and this is the only fucking thing that's helping me. I can't stand going on like this for the rest of my life. Can't you have the decency to see me through it until I get straight?'

The trouble was Rick would drink as well — and so, of course, did I — but usually he'd get paralytic and that's the worst thing you can do with coke. Then you completely lose control and can't handle it.

Sometimes, after Bootleggers, we'd go on to Fandangoes, another club which stayed open until 6.00am.

Fandangoes was fun but usually, after Bootleggers or Stringfellows, we'd fall into a cab and wend our way home. Then there was the problem of getting Rick up the stairs and into the flat. Sometimes the cab driver would help me. Otherwise, I dragged him upstairs as best I could, and dumped him on the couch or the bed.

At last we'd both get to bed but then Rick would wake up saying, 'Oh, I fucking need a wee!' Then he'd stagger up, falling all over the place, and suddenly I'd see him pulling at

Patty Parfitt

the wooden surround of the bed as if he was lifting the lid of the loo.

'Rick, what are you *doing?*'

'I'm going to the loo — get out of the loo!'

'You silly bastard! This is the bedroom!'

We marked the NIPS on a scale of one to five. He usually got to about three, bordering on three and a half. Five meant death!

I think the day Rick wanted to throw himself into the Thames he was on a good four. He was on a real downer of a day. Everything was getting him down — mainly the lack of money. I'd taken a job as a manicurist to bring in a bit of extra cash but Rick made me give it up after six weeks. 'I'm not having my girlfriend going out to work!' It made him look stupid.

Usually when he was feeling miserable I'd take him off to the pub or out shopping to cheer him up. This time I went off to the supermarket and he went to the pub alone and he obviously had more than a couple of halves and a few vodkas. He probably had a few lines as well.

When I got back he was bad, pacing the flat, worse than I'd ever seen him. He was distraught and looked it.

He was rambling 'I've had enough, I've had it, I've really had enough. Marietta's a cow. She said she'd see me broke and she's won. Everybody is against me, the world's against me. Even you probably hate me.'

'Come on, Rick. Calm down. Let's talk about it.'

'No, Patty!'

Then he started rambling about the devil again. Sometimes he used to hear voices.

'It's the devil, Patty. You don't understand, you don't understand at all. I'm fighting him.'

Rick knew that his drinking, coke abuse and fury at being broke were turning him into a bit of a bastard, but he told me that he didn't mean to hurt anyone. It wasn't *him* doing it — it was the voices telling him to.

Laughing All Over The World

They would say to him: 'You've got to look after yourself, Rick, you've got to look after number one, all these other people are only using you because you're famous.'

It was all rubbish, of course. His mum adores him and so do the rest of his family. And me — I adored him even more. But he was totally paranoid. It wasn't the only time it happened. One night he said he actually saw the devil. We were sitting at home at Quay West and he'd been drinking whisky for most of the day.

Suddenly he grabbed me and threw me across the room screaming, 'Get out! The devil's here! Get out or he'll get you too!'

He pinned my arms to my sides and half pushed and half dragged me into the bedroom. Then he slammed the door and locked it. I started hammering on it, crying, 'Rick! Let me out! What's going on?' I was terrified of him. He seemed to have totally lost control.

I could hear him wrecking the sitting room throwing furniture across the room, the sound of glass shattering and Rick grunting as if he was actually having a fist fight with someone. I kept banging at the door begging him to let me out and eventually it went quiet. The key turned in the lock, the door opened and he stood there crying hysterically.

Then he put his arms around me and held me close: 'I've won, Patty. I beat him! I've won!'

After that he seemed to recover and, once I'd cleared up the room, it was: 'Right, let's go out. Time to get changed.'

But the day he went to the Thames was different and I was frightened. Rick had been drinking whisky and it always brought out the worst in him. The only time he was violent was when he drank whisky — that was the only time the devil appeared as well.

This time he said: 'I'm hearing the voices again — I've got to get out. I've got to escape.'

I tried to put my arms around him. 'Don't be silly. Let's have a cup of tea. Or do you want a drink? We could go shopping.'

Patty Parfitt

He went mad then, shouting at the top of his voice. 'I don't want a drink! I've had enough drink. This is what it does to me. Can't you see that? I'm going out. I don't know where I'm going and I won't come back because I'm probably going to kill myself. Don't tell me I'm silly! I'm sick to death of everyone telling me that I'm silly! I'm not silly, I know what I'm doing, but you don't understand and you never will until I'm dead!'

He ran out of the door and I ran after him. I was thinking: 'I know this is a load of bullshit, I know it is, but what if it isn't?' He looked terrible. Totally loony. He was all eyes, big staring eyes, his face was pinched and his hair wilder than usual. He really looked deathly.

He ran down the stairs and I dashed after him. When we reached the hall he headed for the front door with me following along behind.

Suddenly he spun round, grabbed my shoulders, pulled me back into the lobby and slapped me hard around the face.

I was crying. I remember saying: 'I'm not leaving you Rick! You can hit me until I'm black and blue but I'm not leaving you! Let me help you, let's talk this out.'

It was as if he was in a kind of trance. I could see he was about to go for me so I ran back up the stairs and he chased after me. Back in the flat he got hold of me and this time he really hurt me. He punched me hard and said: 'I could fucking kill you any time I want.' He put his hands around my neck and started to choke me. Even then I didn't believe he would but I was terrified, gasping desperately for air.

Then abruptly he stopped and said he was leaving. He was going to throw himself off a bridge — 'Just don't come out after me again or you'll get more of that and next time I won't stop!' With that he punched me in the stomach and I could hear him running down the stairs. I think I was in shock. I didn't know what to do. I managed to get up and rubbed my neck which was so sore. Then I rang Colin Johnson, who was Quo's manager at the time and lived just

Laughing All Over The World

down the road from Francis in Purley on the same grand estate.

Thank God, Colin answered the phone and even I could hear the panic in my voice.

'Get the hell over here, Colin. He's run off and he says he's going to throw himself off Battersea Bridge!'

Colin knew what Rick was like. He didn't need telling twice. He put the phone down and obviously got straight in his Range Rover and headed for our flat in Battersea.

Twenty minutes later Colin arrived and left immediately—returning with a bedraggled Rick in tow who was crying his eyes out again. He started to put his arms around me and was saying 'Sorry, sorry, darling, I'm so sorry. It's those fucking voices telling me to kill myself and I wanted to, not because the voices told me but because I'm no good to anyone.'

Rick was totally shattered, tired out.

I comforted him. 'It's all right now, go and lie down and I'll be in.' When I went to check him a few minutes later he was sleeping like a baby.

I flicked the light off and drew the curtains. Then Colin and I made coffee.

'What the hell was that all about?' I said.

'Do you know where I found him?'

'Well, he wasn't wet and his shoes weren't muddy ...'

'No, I found him sitting on that little beach bit by the river throwing stones into the water. I went up to him and said, "Hello, I heard you were here," and he said, "Oh? Did *she* send you? Did she tell you I was going to kill myself?"'

'"Yeah," I said. "So why the fuck didn't you then?"'

I couldn't understand it — Colin was smiling. He looked as if he was going to burst out laughing.

'Rick said, "Well, I got to the bridge but the tide was out and I would have hurt myself if I'd fallen!"

'"Well, why didn't you go further along the bridge where the water was deeper?"

13

Patty Parfitt

'"There it was too deep and too fast. The current would have pulled me away."'

'"But Rick, you wanted to die."'

Rick apparently thought about that one for a moment.

'"Yeah, I did at the time."'

I said to Colin, 'Well, you don't look very worried.'

'Well, you know where I found him, so now you know why I'm not very worried. Why don't you get it into your head that he's an attention seeker, Patty? Stop giving in to all his silly little whims.'

'But if I don't, then one day something might happen. I can't risk it. I couldn't risk doing that with someone else's life. I'd feel guilty for the rest of my days. He's got me, hasn't he? He's got me and he knows it. He knows I won't let him down but he has to test me all the time.'

The biggest shock of all came at eight o'clock when Rick emerged from the bedroom, a bit bleary-eyed, full of apologies but otherwise remarkably unscathed.

'Right,' he said. 'I'm hungry. Let's go out.' I looked at him in amazement.

'I'm really, really sorry,' he said, 'I didn't mean it and I'll never do it again. I love you darlin'. Don't leave me, because if it wasn't for you I'd die. Come on, give me a kiss and a cuddle. Let's forget all about it, let's have a drink.' He looked at me — and at the welts that were quickly coming up on my neck.

'You'd better wear the black dress and the black choker around your neck or something. Come on. Don't bang on about it, Patty. If you harp on something, Patty, it will harp on you for the rest of your life.'

Stunned, I went to get changed while Rick had a couple of Nikis. Then off we went to the Italian as usual.

I sipped a glass of mineral water but, every time I swallowed, it hurt. Rick, in contrast, was fine, chatting to everyone and super-attentive to me.

'Isn't she gorgeous? Isn't she a darlin'? Champagne I think, darlin',' he said, looking around the table.

Oh God, I thought. Here we go and here we go and here we go — again!

2

So Ends Another Life

In 1965 Butlins was a very groovy place to be and the four sixteen-year-old boys who got off the London train at Minehead were determined to make the most of it. The group — Francis Rossi, his school chums Alan Lancaster and John Coghlan and junior organist Roy Lynes — called themselves The Spectres and playing the four month summer season at the holiday camp was a major step forward in their ambition to become world famous superstars.

Just out of school, liberated at last, they were hired to play two sets a day, one in the afternoon and a repeat performance of three hours every evening. But that left plenty of time to sample the booze, meet and greet the numerous chicks in their tight ribbed sweaters and mini skirts and, hopefully, please God, even get their respective legs over.

Francis scored before he'd even had a chance to deposit his guitar in the chalet. He met Jean as she was waiting with her sister at the gates of the camp to sign in. She was one hot

Patty Parfitt

chick: skinny, about 5' 5", attractive, dark-haired and definitely trendy — and that mattered. It was admiration and lust at first sight.

In those days, Francis preferred to call himself Mike. It was always assumed that when he left school he'd go into the ice cream business like his grandfather but his Italian–Irish parents made the mistake of giving him his first guitar when he was seven and that was that.

He met Alan Lancaster when he arrived at Sedgehill School after leaving a Catholic junior school and, like Alan, he quickly joined the school orchestra, also playing the trumpet.

Alan Lancaster with his friend Alan Key soon teamed up with Francis and one day they all went off to a party in Peckham, each secretly hoping to get off with a girl called Margaret.

But once there she didn't hold their attention for long. A small group were playing at the party and the three boys were entranced and decided there and then to form a band.

That summer, in 1962, Francis and Alan Lancaster were taken by Alan's mum and dad on holiday to Butlins at Clacton. Watching the resident camp band bashing out their version of that summer's biggest hit, 'Telstar' by The Tornados — an instrumental featuring an organ — gave the boys another brainwave; they needed an organ in the band too. The search for an organist began, and the seed that would become Status Quo was sown.

Like Francis, Alan had become hooked on music young. He was given his first guitar — a second hand job which set his mum and dad back five pounds — when he was about nine. He spent hours trying to play it with little success and finally — way ahead of his time and showing signs of the rock star to come — smashed it up in frustration.

But once he joined the school orchestra he became music mad. But then Francis fell out with Alan Key and Alan left the 'band'. But the search for an organist went on.

Classmate Jess Jaworski, who impressed the youthful rockers

Laughing All Over The World

because he'd been given a £70 guitar by his parents, was the ideal candidate, especially since he was prepared to take his guitar back to the shop and swop it for an organ and a small Vox AC 30 amplifier.

A variety of mates helped out when necessary on drums and, after driving the neighbours mad with their rehearsals in Alan's upstairs bedroom, the group were ready for their first gig at the Samuel Jones Sports Club, Lordship Lane, Dulwich, which was arranged for them by Alan's dad. They played five numbers, took a break, then played them all again in a different order and, thanks to a whip-round from the regulars, they earned the princely sum of about £4.

Because of the racket they were making in Alan's bedroom, they were forced to rehearse at the nearby Air Cadets headquarters. And that's where the boys met music-mad sixteen-year-old John Coghlan who had been bashing away at the drums for as long as his parents could remember and was rehearsing with his own group in a next door room. He'd already left school and wanted to become a mechanic but music was his first love and he was impressed when he heard The Spectres.

The boys thought that John's group were crap but they liked his heavy, hard drumming.

In no time he was recruited, too, and after that the boys never stopped rehearsing. John's father called them the League of Nations: there was a Pole (Jess), an Italian (Francis), a half-Scot (John's dad came from Glasgow) and a Cockney (Alan).

Although they were only fifteen the boys managed to get an increasing number of gigs thanks to Alan's dad who acted as their unofficial manager. Francis' dad helped too: he drove them to the various clubs and halls in his ice cream van but this did bring problems. The police, spotting a group of adolescent boys careering around South London in an ice cream van packed with musical equipment, were constantly stopping them.

Soon they were spotted by local gas-fitter Pat Barlow. He

Patty Parfitt

had contacts in the music business and was keen to become their manager.

As a result, gig after gig followed so that often the boys were getting home at four in the morning. Then they had to struggle up for school the next day at 7.30am. Most of the time they coped by skipping lessons and escaping to the music room for a kip or they slept at their desks with textbooks propped up in front of them.

But they were all convinced they were going to make it big time and Francis was certain of it. Music had always been his life, and he was determined to snatch his dream while he could.

Thanks to Pat Barlow the boys played at the Orpington Civic Hall supporting The Hollies — this was nearly, almost the big time — and Pat also managed to get them their audition for the Butlins summer season. Alan and Francis couldn't wait to leave school and get out there.

Only Jess the organist chose not to go to Butlins. A sensible boy, he decided to stay on at school to take his A Levels and then went on to Exeter University. He later became a computer consultant. But the boys quickly found a replacement for him in Roy Lynes, another music nut who'd been playing pub gigs with bands in Redhill, Surrey. So the boys arrived at Butlins full of hope.

It was great, but something else happened at Butlins which was to change the future of The Spectres. Before long the boys bumped into the camp's boy wonder, a sixteen-year-old blonde boy called Richard Parfitt. He called himself Ricky Harrison and had also been hired for the summer season. He was appearing in a cabaret trio with two identical twins, Jean and Gloria, both skinny, cockney brunettes with bouffant hairdos. The trio called themselves The Highlights.

Ricky obviously had a 'thing' going with Jean — and hinted that he'd been with Gloria, too, and the lads were naturally impressed. Until recently, they were still in touch with Rick and even did a couple of numbers on some Quo gigs until one night, in the Holiday Inn, Manchester, after the show, they overheard Rick saying: 'When are those fucking twins going to go?' The girls retired hurt, and never contacted him again.

But at Butlins in the good old days Rick had a lot in common with the other lads. Like them he'd started young. His mum, Lil, bought her only son a piano when he was seven and a guitar when he was ten, and by then he had his heart set on a career in showbusiness.

All in all Ricky's track record was pretty impressive. He'd even been on television at the tender age of eleven on the pop show *Midwinter Music* hosted by Steve Race, singing the Cliff Richard number 'Travellin' Light'. At the age of twelve, he was earning his own money from his showbiz career, helped as always by his parents' continuous support.

His dad, Dick, got him gigs and really started him in the business. But, being a sensible boy from a good family, Ricky's fame didn't go to his head — at least not then — and he stayed on at school until he was fifteen. If music was his first love, sport came a very close second and he played cricket and rugby with enthusiasm and captained the school football team.

An intellectual he was not, but the girls, especially me, loved his blonde hair and runner bean figure, so fashionable at the time, and the lads enjoyed his easy-going sense of humour and admired his confidence and charm.

Francis was suspicious of him — his clothes and tiny bum made him think Rick was gay. But the Italian macho boy soon discovered that his fears were groundless.

The boys and Ricky became good friends — especially Ricky, Francis and Alan Lancaster — but at the end of the summer season they went their separate ways — Rick back to Woking and the boys to Peckham where they carried on plugging away at their music.

The music scene was changing fast and the boys found the current craze for soul records like 'Midnight Hour' and 'It Takes Two' had dimmed their rising star. Getting a gig with

Patty Parfitt

their old style was proving difficult.

But their enthusiasm was as strong as ever — if they could just hang on, they were sure a recording contract lay just around the corner.

Auditions came and went, Pat Barlow worked his socks off and finally a contact of his, songwriter Ronnie Scott who'd been writing songs with rock 'n' roller Marty Wilde, was impressed enough to play one of their tapes to a guy called John Schroeder, who was then a talent scout for the Piccadilly label.

Schroeder liked what he heard and Pat drove the boys up to audition in front of him at Charlie Chester's Casino.

He also turned up to watch the boys rehearse at Pat's showroom which was a tiny space full of packing cases and, at last, the boys won their recording contract.

On July 18, 1966 Pye records (who'd recently bought Piccadilly) signed up The Spectres — Alan Lancaster, Francis Rossi, John Coghlan and Roy Lynes — for a possible five-year run.

They all chucked in their part-time jobs, dreamed of all the money that was about to come their way and waited for the stardom and the glamour that would inevitably accompany their first hit.

And they waited. And they waited.

Their first single 'I (Who have Nothing)' did just that — nothing. The second, an Alan Lancaster song called the 'Hurdy Gurdy Man' released before Christmas in 1966, bombed too. But the boys weren't discouraged. As always they had amazing faith in themselves.

Schroeder continued to support them but their next single '(We Ain't Got) Nothing Yet' flopped again although it did get a few mentions in the music press.

Drastic measures were called for and the boys decided that they'd had enough of The Spectres. Flower power and the new psychedelic sound in fashion at the time demanded a new name and they hit on Traffic.

Laughing All Over The World

They liked the sound of it and, completely unintentionally, they had also found a way to get themselves some publicity. Stevie Winwood had just split from the Spencer Davis Group and had formed his own band — also called Traffic — on the Island label. What's more he was currently chugging up the charts with Traffic's first hit, 'Single Paper Sun'.

Winwood was not amused by this bunch of young upstarts who were calling themselves by the same name. And even when they diplomatically changed the name again to Traffic Jam he complained that it was still far too similar.

What with one thing and another the band seemed to be getting nowhere fast. Schroeder was concerned that their sound wasn't the sound that was beginning to blossom in the late Sixties. The boys just carried on rehearsing regardless until Pat came up with yet another brain wave — they'd have to change their name again.

Status Quo was a phrase that Pat kept reading in the newspaper in one context or another and it stuck in his mind. The boys liked it but it had to be The Status Quo.

The boys went back into the studio towards the end of 1967. They'd already recorded what they thought would be their next single, 'Gentleman Joe's Sidewalk Cafe', and were about to start work on one of Francis' songs called 'Pictures of Matchstick Men'. John Schroeder was pleased with the group but he was keen to boost the vocals so they started looking around for a vocalist to join Quo.

There was one obvious choice — their old mate from Butlins, Ricky Parfitt, who, by good fortune, had just had a bust-up with the girls in The Highlights.

So Ricky duly joined the band just in time to record 'Pictures of Matchstick Men'.

True to form, Pat Barlow went all out to make 'Matchstick Men' a hit. He was still running his small central heating business in South London as well as acting as Quo's part-time manager and now he acquired a partner called Joe Bunce.

Joe was a customer of Pat's, he had the same belief in the

25

Patty Parfitt

band that Pat had, but he had something that Pat didn't have — money. Pat's efforts in the past to get Quo to the top of the charts had been enthusiastic to say the least but not always successful — or very cool.

Pat put his heart into promoting the band, but still had his central heating business to run. As a result he often arrived for meetings with promoters clad in his overalls. This didn't help the cool image the Quo were trying to create.

But now, armed with Joe's dosh, they were able to buy airplay time for 'Matchstick Men' on the groovy pirate radio station Radio Caroline. The song caught the psychedelic mood of the Sixties, it was played on Caroline two or three times a day and soon it charted reaching number seven. It did well in America, too, reaching number 18.

The boys quickly discovered that once you had a hit life changed considerably. You could appear as rebellious as you liked on stage but off you were expected to do as you were told and conform to the rules.

To their horror, they were carted off to Carnaby Street, then the centre of 'Swinging London', to buy their stage clothes. Frilly shirts, satin trousers and new shoes were *de rigueur* as were the new, slightly effeminate, highly lacquered hairdos. The boys found these slightly embarrassing but they were enjoying the limelight, especially the TV shows.

Now they'd finally got that elusive hit they were convinced that the only way was up. They were, unfortunately, wrong.

Their next single, 'Black Veils of Melancholy', sank without trace. The following one, 'Ice in the Sun', made it to number ten in the charts and everyone heaved a sigh of relief. But while 'Matchstick Men' was a flower power, psychedelic sort of sound, 'Ice in the Sun' was an out and out pop song and when the band played live they didn't really fit either mould. Then they were just ... Quo. That was their true identity but it took them some years to see that. In the meantime, their popularity dwindled.

1969 was a year when the band had no hit at all and, if you

didn't have a hit, getting a gig was difficult. The boys were learning hard and fast that the music business was just that — a business, and a ruthless one, too. Fame, they discovered was fleeting, fortune even more so. Money was short and and things got worse when the record company hired a roadie to look after them, John Fanning from Liverpool.

Far from being there at the boys' beck and call, John was very much the boss. For a start, he earned £30 a week while they were only on £19 a week each and what he said went. Wages were stopped as punishment for misdemeanours — it certainly wasn't the rock 'n' roll lifestyle the boys expected.

The band supported some big names — Madeleine Bell, Gene Pitney and appeared with Amen Corner, Love Affair and The Herd, whose keyboard player, Andy Bown late joined Quo.

Times were hard but still the band kept going — getting gigs where they could and searching for a musical identity. On reflection, they had one big thing going for them — unlike other pop bands of the time, and despite their age, they had been through the mill, they were hardened professionals rather than a manufactured band just put together to mime on *Top of the Pops*.

They were prepared to persevere, they had faith in themselves and they were still hugely ambitious.

Pat Barlow and Joe Bunce were still managing the band but, because of their other commitments, were reluctant to manage Quo full time, so much of the organisation and keeping the boys in order went to John Fanning.

Despite all the problems, the band still got on well and still gelled as a unit. They took great pride in having their own code, a certain way of talking so no one else knew what they were talking about. It was like still being at school and Francis and Rick enjoyed it immensely. It had its useful side too, especially later on. If one of the band got too cocky, or too big for their plimsolls, the rest would rip them to shreds.

The group kept making records but most sank without trace.

Patty Parfitt

They knew they had become unfashionable but they weren't sure how or why.

Still they kept going and gradually their style was changing. But it was tough and the money was shorter than ever.

In 1969 they were supporting Gene Pitney at the Hammersmith Odeon, when the band Amen Corner popped backstage to say hello. With them was Bob Young who had played with a small band called Attack. They offered him a job as roadie and banker on the grand salary of £15 a week. It wasn't much but it was £5 a week more than Bob had been offered by Jethro Tull, so he accepted with alacrity.

Bob fitted in well, he shared the group's filthy sense of humour and began to write songs with them. But, as success seemed more elusive than ever, the atmosphere within the Quo's 'management' began to change. There were arguments. Pat Barlow was still managing the band part-time but he was becoming increasingly exasperated by the music business — and by Quo.

Francis tried acting as peacemaker — but without much success, and anyway much of the problem was to do with money — or the lack of it. The band were so broke they sent their wives and girlfriends out to work and their ever-supportive Mums and Dads helped out.

Bob decided to try and get the band signed with another record label and approached Peter Prince, the head of A and R at MCA records.

The problem was that Peter Prince, although impressed, then moved to Pye Records, the label the band wanted to leave and the one which had firmly classed them as a pop band. But Prince persuaded them to stay on and for a while it looked as if things were on the up.

The arguments with Pat Barlow rumbled on and the band decided that, although they wanted to keep him on, they wanted rid of Joe Bunce. What they really needed was a proper full-time manager but they felt a certain loyalty to Pat.

Laughing All Over The World

But they were growing up and Pat and Joe were unfashionable, the worst sin of all. Something would have to give.

Then Roy Lynes, the organist, decided to quit, and emigrated to New Zealand with his wife.

So then there were four. The band set about playing their harder sound at clubs and pubs. The Carnaby Street clothes went — they were uncomfortable, and the boys couldn't afford them now anyway. Instead they wore jeans and looked as scruffy as possible. Their hair was now seriously long.

At the time, this was regarded as shocking behaviour. A band was supposed to dress up to go on stage. But, by now, they had sunk so low that they thought that they might as well do as they liked — they had very little to lose.

But the change of image, together with the hardening of the sound on stage, seemed to give the band a new lease of life.

They felt more natural and the music was coming more naturally, too. In fact, despite the fact they were still skint, they began to enjoy themselves again. They'd tried everything in pursuit of fame from violins to Bee Gees-style harmonising and now they just played what they wanted to play — hard rock 'n' roll.

Ma Kelly's Greasy Spoon — with Ricky's nan's café firmly in mind — was their third album for Pye. They wrote most of the songs themselves and one — a blues song called 'Down the Dustpipe' — gave them their first hit for over a year. It took off slowly and Tony Blackburn — never a hard rock 'n' roll fan — was heard to tell his listeners: 'Down the dustbin with this one.' But despite that, and the sneers of other critics, it made its way up to number 12 in the charts. Not great, but much better.

Quo were on their way back.

The non-events of the previous years had made the boys toughen up. They began to do their own thing, giving the two-fingered salute to anyone who disagreed. They couldn't give a shit — at least on the surface.

Patty Parfitt

And still the music press ignored them. In true Quo fashion, they pressed on, slowly but surely building up a good following. In November 1970 they followed up 'Down the Dustpipe' with another hit 'In My Chair'. It was still the hippy era of peace and love but Quo, with their cockiness and 'don't care' attitude, had begun to make people sit up and take notice.

The boys appeared on *Top of the Pops* and shook their long hair around more than ever.

People still remembered the tinkly sound of 'Pictures of Matchstick Men' but their next album, *Dog of Two Head* showed how far they'd come. It wasn't a big hit but it didn't fade without trace either.

John Peel played it on Radio One and Kid Jensen on Radio Luxembourg, then a very in station to tune in to.

The lads were invited over to record a special live session for the station at the Blow Up Club which was a huge success, so good that Kid Jensen later confessed that he'd ended up on stage with them singing 'Bye Bye Johnny'.

Quo could sense that the big time was almost within their grasp. And they were hungrier than ever for it. But they knew that for it to happen there had to be some changes.

The ever-faithful Pat Barlow and Joe Bunce simply weren't big-time people. Therefore they had to go.

The band fired them. Pat and Joe must have felt very hurt and let down by the lads they'd worked so hard for. But Quo, and Francis and Rick in particular, knew they had to be ruthless to get on in the music business. And they were so close ...

For the next 18 months they flirted with different managers but they really wanted Colin Johnson who'd worked as a talent booker with the NEMS agency but now had set up on his own.

Colin joined Quo in a roundabout way. He'd bumped into them around the circuit but there was a girl he was friendly with who worked for Pye Records. Every time a tape of a new band came in to Pye which she thought he'd like she'd send it

Laughing All Over The World

on. In one package she sent him two: The Foundations singing 'Now That I Found You' and Quo's 'Pictures of Matchstick Men'. He was anxious to sign both and called Marlow and Bunce. Colin said how much he liked Status Quo and signed them on the spot.

But it wasn't as easy as that. Not long afterwards he got a call from agent Arthur Howes.

'Have you got a contract with Status Quo?' he said. 'Well, tear it up, lad. I've got them under contract for another two years.' So that was that.

Colin said that if anything went wrong Quo could ring him, and when their contract was over Francis, who Colin had always got on with, phoned.

'We're in a bit of trouble — can we come and see you?'

The answer was yes. Francis and Rick brought their tour manager Bob Young with them, whose songwriting skill was invaluable to Quo.

The meeting between Quo and Johnson was crucial. Rossi explained although they'd had two hits they'd now changed their style — and couldn't get any gigs as a result. And they didn't want to play the same boring circuit, they wanted to branch out.

Johnson took over as their agent.

Three months later the boys came back saying: 'We're not happy with our management. We want you to manage us.'

Colin Johnson said that he couldn't get rid of Pat and Joe Bunce — the boys had to do it themselves.

Rossi and Rick preferred other people to do their dirty work for them and always shied away from any kind of confrontation. But it had to be done. They bit the bullet — but took the coward's way out, with a letter.

Then they went back to Colin Johnson who immediately became their manager. He had total faith in them.

But Quo were broke. What they didn't know was that Colin Johnson was, too. But he trotted down to the bank, re-mortgaged his house for £8,000 and invested it in Status Quo.

Patty Parfitt

Colin became manager, agent, publisher, public relations officer — and everything in between.

Colin was shrewd and knew the music business inside out. But more than that, he believed in the band absolutely. He knew that their greatest strength was their live performances.

He set to work, getting Quo any gig he could, and even subbing them from his own pocket. He got them out and about, gigging everywhere — and they began to attract a following.

The boys impressed the music biz people they met. They were always laughing, joking about, always a lot of fun. They took the piss out of everyone, including Johnson. But, underneath, they were fiercely ambitious, especially Rossi. He took his music seriously — he wanted to make music, make a good living and look after his family. Rick just wanted to be a superstar and own a fleet of cars, while John 'Spud' Coghlan was enjoying a world of his own, and all the trappings of rock stardom. Alan Lancaster was ambitious, too, but jealous of Rossi for fronting the band. He was the one who'd started the band after all.

But they got along together happily enough and, as the hits began and the money started to roll in, they felt even better.

When they got their record deal with Phonogram they were all thrilled. They were young but they impressed the record company with their professionalism. As a band they were totally reliable, always well rehearsed, and very consistent.

Soon the boys started making good money — much to their collective glee. Johnson managed to sign them with Billy Gaff who managed Rod Stewart and Rory Gallagher. Rick was very impressed with himself. If there was one person he wanted to be it was Rod Stewart.

Janet, the married lover and Rick's then girlfriend, didn't help much either. She thought Rick should be a much bigger star than he was and didn't mind saying so.

The Quo were still pretty much the same, despite all the attention, but Rick in particular lapped it all up. Once, en route to LWT for an interview he embarrassed an executive with them by winding down the window of the limo and shouting at a cyclist: 'You know who we are, don't you?'

'Fuck off,' said the cyclist.

Rick wound the window up looking hurt.

'Well,' he said to the others. 'That wasn't very nice was it!'

3

You're Just What I Was Looking For Today

Francis married Jean whom he'd met at the gates of Butlins, Alan married Pat, a dark and petite Eastender, John Coghlan had a long-term girlfriend, Linda. This left Rick. He was footloose and fancy-free and relishing every minute of it — kind of. Apart from the occasional groupie, the others had settled happily into domesticity but Rick was still Jack the Lad.

There had been The Highlights, of course, but that was ages ago. And, more importantly, there was Janet, the older woman, married, of course, but sexually she brought him a satisfaction that previously he'd only fantasised about. She boosted his ego.

But, of course, there wasn't any future in it. She was more than ten years older, she was married, and they were close, but it couldn't be anything more.

So he cruised Woking in his Jag, showing off and posing

Patty Parfitt

nonchalantly in the local working men's club.

As he told me later, I had already caught his eye. I lived just up the road, and our parents knew each other. I was only just eighteen. Pretty, bottle blonde and a challenge, that's how Rick saw it — and he couldn't resist.

I heard about Ricky Parfitt long before I met him. He was only 21 but he was already very big in Woking. Everyone knew Ricky Parfitt from the Sheerwater estate who'd had a hit with Status Quo and 'Pictures of Matchstick Men'. Despite the fame and glory Ricky was still living with his Mum, Lil, and his Dad, Dick, in a council flat. His Dad was an insurance collector — a real ladies' man. His Mum worked part-time in a bakers' and a wallpaper shop.

Like me, he'd lived in Woking as a kid. Then the family moved away and came back when Ricky was ten. He went to Westfields School on one side of town and I went to Sheerwater Secondary on the other, but us girls never mixed with boys from Westfields — they were all a bit rough. That's why Lil wanted to move to Sheerwater.

It was a council estate but much nicer in those days. Lily and my Mum, Daisy, knew each other and Ricky's Dad, and my Dad, Stan, used to see each other in the local community club.

Ricky is an only child and his Mum adores him. He adores her, too. 'My Ricky', as Lil calls him, can do no wrong and she is desperately proud of his success as a pop star.

'You must get your Patricia to meet my Ricky,' she'd say to Mum and she'd come home and say, 'Ricky Parfitt came down the club today. Why don't you come down and meet him? He's such a nice boy.'

Everyone thought he was great and he drew admiring glances wherever he drove, in his flashy Jaguar BPB 783B which he'd bought from the local doctor. Playing in the band, posing in his car and playing snooker seemed to occupy most of his time.

Laughing All Over The World

But for some reason I didn't really want to meet him. I stayed well clear and walked in the opposite direction whenever I clocked the Jaguar. Perhaps I subconsciously knew that it would only lead to trouble. Anyway, I was keen on someone else at the time, a chap called Andy. I'd left school at fifteen and I was working as a receptionist at Efco chemical company and Andy was one of the chemists there. He was a gorgeous blond, although, unfortunately, he had another girlfriend as well as me.

But apparently this 'great' guy Ricky Parfitt often saw me walking around Woking as he cruised up and down the main drag past Woolworths and the bus stop. He liked my long blonde hair — Ricky has always been a sucker for blondes. It was inevitable that our paths would cross eventually and it happened outside the local butcher's. I'd gone to collect Mum from the shops and she was there having a chat with Lil. Suddenly I saw Rick approaching in the Jag and, instinctively, I jumped back in my dad's 1100, told Mum I had to go to buy a *New Musical Express* and roared off.

Ricky followed in hot pursuit and we had a car chase through Woking. He was closing on me but I stamped on the accelerator and craftily managed to do a swift right turn and stop while he carried on roaring down the road. Then I drove back to Sheerwater while he drove around Woking searching for me! It was all very silly but my heart was pounding away. I went back to pick up Mum and he was there again, but this time he didn't stop, but just looked over at me and drove off. I noticed his hair first. Long, very long, with a slight wave and blonde. Quite a nice face. Big nose. Interesting smile.

That evening he cruised up and down my street for about half an hour. And the next evening. And the next. It went on for a whole week. I never went out but I used to wait for him to drive by, and then sneak a look from behind the curtains.

Patty Parfitt

My mum told me to stop being so silly and she'd creep up behind me and fling the curtains wide open, and I'd shriek and run upstairs. Anyway, I began to think: 'Well, he's quite nice really!' Andy had someone else anyway. Then one night he didn't turn up and I thought: 'Bloody cheek!' When he didn't turn up for two whole evenings I felt quite disappointed.

But then the phone rang.

'I'm a friend of Rick's,' said a man's voice. 'He wants to go out with you.'

'I don't want to.'

'Well, please call him, and put him out of his misery because he's driving me mad!'

So, feeling very cool, I rang him up. His Dad answered and said Ricky wasn't in — he'd popped out to get a curry, but would be back soon.

'Can you let him know I've rung? Do you want my number?'

'What, your number?! He doesn't need that, love — it's plastered all over his wall!'

Ricky rang back within half an hour and asked me out. Later he told me he'd never been so nervous with anyone in his life as he was with me then.

I said, 'Oh, all right then, when?'

'What are you doing now?'

'I've got to do some things for Mum.' Of course I hadn't really.

'What about tomorrow?'

'OK.'

'I'll pick you up at half past seven.'

He was there on the dot of half past seven. I don't know how he manages it but he's never late and he's rarely early, he's almost always dead on time — and, as I discovered later, God help you if you're not.

I dressed with care: a black mini skirt, a shocking pink

blouse and what Ricky called my Minnie Mouse shoes, which were white plastic with big chunky heels.

He turned up — in the Jag, of course — in an old pair of jeans covered in strategically placed patches, a T-shirt, yellow boots and a patchwork leather jacket which was all ripped under the arms.

I slid into the front seat and he was shy.

'Where do you want to go?'

'I don't know — *you're* taking *me* out.'

'Shall we go to a pub or something? What pub do you want to go to?'

'I don't know, I don't go to pubs.'

'We can't go to the local one because I've known them all in there since I was five.'

So we ended up going to Ottershaw to The Bleak House. I still remember the cosy open fire, the fish tank. I can still hear our conversation:

'Nice red fish.'

'The blue ones are nice too.'

I still remember that excited but nervous feeling I had that night. He drank Scotch and Coke, so I did, too, because I didn't know what else to have and, basically, we just sat there making awkward conversation and then he took me home.

I was really nervous. To make matters worse Mum and Dad were hanging out of the window staring and so, it seemed, were half the neighbours. I couldn't wait to get out of the car.

But I sat. Was he going to kiss me goodnight or what?

'Can I take you out tomorrow?'

'OK. Well, you can kiss me if you want, Ricky Parfitt!'

'Oh, thanks,' he said and gave me a peck on the cheek!

The next day he picked me up and took me to the working men's club in Woking where his dad was a member. He and his dad were into snooker in a big way and he said: 'I'd like you to come and watch me play snooker.'

Patty Parfitt

Of course, I said yes. It wasn't my idea of a romantic evening out but I learned a bit more about Ricky in the process. He was playing with his best friend Peter Gibb, a really nice chap who worked in advertising in London.

'I'll thrash him,' said Ricky confidently. We had a couple of drinks and I sat down to watch.

'No,' said Rick. 'You sit over there, up there on that stool. It's a bit awkward if you sit where you are now because you'll put people off their game.'

So I dutifully moved and sat on the stool in my mini skirt and my stretch pull-on PVC boots.

Ricky did thrash him and he was very pleased with himself. 'I told you I would.'

'Well, you can buy the drinks then,' said Peter and Ricky went off to get them.

'Peter, I'm sorry if I put you off,' I said.

Peter laughed.

'No, don't worry, you didn't. Rick always makes the girls sit up there so he can see up their skirts. Because when you're sitting up there he can see your knickers every time he bends over the cue.' I laughed. It seemed funny then — not so funny later.

Rick drove me home and this time I thought he was bound to kiss me properly. But it was just another peck on the cheek and 'See you tomorrow.'

We met every night and, within a week, I'd fallen for him. If it hadn't been for the fact that all I got was a peck on the cheek, I would have thought he'd fallen for me, too.

Shortly afterwards he asked me to take him to the airport one day. Quo were going to Northern Ireland to play a few gigs. I was scared — he was, too. There was a lot of trouble over there at that time and on the day he went the two British soldiers had been shot dead; then the trouble really began in earnest.

He called me from the hotel before one of the gigs.

'Patty, it's really scary over here. All the equipment has been searched at least a dozen times and we even have a couple of guards minding us at the pub where we're playing.

'Last night we didn't even do an encore but came straight back to the hotel. I thought I'd never see you again — I thought I was going to be blown up or shot.'

We chatted for a while and I promised to meet him at the airport when the band arrived back home. Meanwhile I was under orders to buy some jeans and get some white plimsolls. That was the essential Quo outfit.

Perhaps it wasn't love but, by now, I was very keen. I thought he was lovely, and I was very excited about meeting him at the airport. So excited that I bought him a new pair of leather driving gloves which set me back twenty pounds — almost a whole week's wages.

It was the first time I'd met the band, too. Francis was the first one I spotted. He was very skinny and he seemed to me much taller than he does now, probably because he's put on weight since. In fact, he's only about 5' 9".

They all had really, really long hair. Francis was a bit casual and distant but Alan Lancaster came up to me immediately and we hit it off straight away. He was really friendly and always smiling, he's a fun bloke and he's always joking around.

He said: 'My wife's called Pat, too — we'll have to do something about that.'

'She's called Patty,' said Rick. In fact, my real name is Patricia-Ann, but Rick had started to call me Patty straight off and I liked it.

'I was thinking of changing my wife's name to Patty. It's nicer,' said Alan.

'No you won't! Your wife's Pat and this is my Patty.'

And suddenly Rick and Alan were involved in this stupid

Patty Parfitt

row about my name. At first I thought they were joking but it soon became apparent that they weren't.

Alan was saying: 'Oh come on, let me. Pat's my wife and you've only just met this girl, although she is lovely ...' And he gave me a beaming smile.

However, I stopped Ricky from bickering with Alan by giving him his present. He loved the gloves — his old ones were terrible, all ripped and held together by staples.

'Great!' he said, and then, to my amazement, he put them on and proceeded to bite a couple of holes in the fingers and ripped them a bit. Then he rubbed them on the floor so they looked dirty and worn!

'They're great, really great, thanks. But they've got to be worn in. I hate anything that's all new looking!' Then he trod all over my new plimsolls so they wouldn't be too white!

'Right, we're leaving.'

As we walked out of the airport I asked: 'What was that all about with you and Alan?'

'Nothing,' he said. 'It's all right. You're Patty and she's Pat and that's that.'

A few days later the band played a gig at the Royal Lancaster Hotel in London — Rick still owes me for the parking ticket. Then, a few days later they played a pub called the Toby Jug in Surrey. I'd never been to a pub gig before and it was fantastic. They were incredibly loud, and you couldn't make out one song from another sometimes, but everyone loved them.

In fact, they went down brilliantly at all their gigs. But there were a few who didn't like their new sound, or who wanted to take the piss of their 'Pictures of Matchstick Men' days. They had a problem with one or two student gigs but they handled it brilliantly. At one in Coventry they were playing their new rock set and two idiots in the audience kept shouting out '"Pictures of Matchstick Men"! "Pictures of Matchstick Men"!'

Laughing All Over The World

In other words, 'You're crap.'

The band just carried on playing louder and louder until they couldn't stand it any longer and Francis said: 'Stop!'

He put his guitar down, and said to the two men: 'OK, come on then — you sing it!'

Mal and Paul, two of the roadies came over and grabbed them. They were frogmarched onto the stage and sat down.

'Come on then,' said Francis. 'You wanted to sing it — so sing it!' Everyone was laughing and these guys were so embarrassed, they made such fools of themselves.

After a while Ricky and Francis put them out of their misery and said to the audience: 'Go on, give them a hand. Right, can we play the gig now?' They played without any more interruptions.

Meanwhile Ricky and I were becoming closer and closer but, much to my dismay, he was still the perfect gentleman. We'd progressed to a snog but that was it.

He used to come round to my house when Mum and Dad were out and we'd watch *Pot Black*, the snooker programme. In fact, now I come to think of it, if you loved Rick, snooker was compulsory.

Ricky was so sweet and I was crazy about him — but still we had moved no further on from snogging. It was pretty obvious I wanted to go further but he kept saying: 'When the time's right. It's better to wait.' And I thought: 'Isn't he nice ...' and I fell deeper and deeper.

One night we were kissing and cuddling in his bedroom, which was more like a cupboard with just room for a single bed and little else, when he suddenly said:

'Well, I suppose we'd better get married then.'

I was thrilled to bits and said: 'OK,' without even thinking about it. It occurred to me that I must love him to respond so quickly.

'Congratulations,' he said and shook my hand and we both

Patty Parfitt

laughed. 'You'd better go and tell your Mum and Dad. I'll come round tomorrow.'

I found Mum in the kitchen preparing the dinner.

'Mum, Ricky and I are getting married.'

She carried on peeling the potatoes.

'Oh, that's nice.'

'Didn't you hear me? I said, Ricky and I are getting married.'

Dad joined us. 'Mmm, that's nice,' he said.

'Are you sure about this?' said Mum.

'Very.'

'I think you both ought to come round and have a talk,' said Dad.

Ricky's Mum and Dad came the next day as well. We all had tea and everything was fine. They were really happy for us, and that night, in Ricky's little bedroom, we made love for the first time.

'The time is right now,' said Rick. 'Now that we we're engaged.'

I was the right girl and he'd wanted to wait until it really meant something to both of us. I'd like to say that the eiderdown really moved but it wasn't a wonderful success, quick and not particularly satisfying. Even so, I was in heaven, Ricky was the best man ever and the world was a wonderful place. Our parents took us down to the club and we had our first dance together with everyone there clapping — and Ricky kicking hell out of my ankles.

The night after Rick proposed to me the band were playing a gig at The Winning Post pub in Twickenham. We told everyone in the dressing room and Francis said, 'Well, we've got to tell the fans about this one. I'll make an announcement on stage. Great!'

And he did — but not in the way we thought he would.

'Quiet, quiet!' Francis shouted from the stage. 'I've got

some announcements to make ... First, my wife's having a baby ...'

Cheers from the crowd.

'And Bob Young's wife Sue is expecting a baby ...'

More cheers.

'And, finally, Rick here and Patty have just got engaged!'

Applause all round. But Rick was livid. He looked over at me and shook his head. Typical Francis, he'd topped Rick again and it was meant to be our night. The rivalry was there even then.

But I didn't care. I was happy. Of course, later on I found out about all the groupies Rick had been with while he was playing gigs out of town, not to mention Janet whom he'd been having an affair with for donkey's years. But ignorance was bliss, and Ricky could do no wrong, even though I was still waiting for my engagement ring. 'We don't need material things,' said Ricky, 'apart from cars!' and he bought a new white Mini Cooper S on HP which we called 'The Min'.

This was before Quo really took off, and money was tight. But the band were all great mates, and Rick and Francis got on well, too — the days of ludicrous rivalries and crazy jealousy between Rick and Francis were well in the future.

It was a happy time. I was happy, and so was Rick. I adored him. He was very funny, he made me smile and laugh a lot.

He always comes across as a very nice genuine chap, witty and very straight to the point. He loves being famous — and he's a very good rock star. He never refuses to give autographs or to speak to people if they come up to him. The only time he ever gets slightly annoyed is if he's in a restaurant and someone interrupts his meal. But even then he's always extremely polite and he'll say something like: 'Look, I'm just enjoying my meal with my girlfriend. Come up and see me when we've finished, as we're going ...'

Patty Parfitt

He keeps up the image of the nice, friendly bloke next door. He always has and, as a result, just about everyone who meets him loves him and warms to him. Then they get to know him!

I never got an engagement ring in the end but I didn't care. After all, he did give me a stone we found on a beach on Hayling Island as a love token!

We got into a routine. I went to all the London gigs and sat there watching him with adoration. The band would travel together, then I'd follow in my dad's car or in The Min.

I couldn't have been happier until one day Rick decided to go and play snooker with his dad at the club. By this time he didn't want me around there — it was men's time, a match, and he didn't like me chatting to other men in the club — so I thought I'd go and see Linda, John's girlfriend.

She was out so I sat in the car waiting for her.

I was just sitting there daydreaming, when I saw a piece of paper poking out from under the front seat. I picked it up and saw it was a letter, a letter which started 'My darling Rick ...' I remember feeling a bit sick but I read on.

It was from Janet, the married woman he'd been having an affair with. I looked at the date — it was some weeks after we'd started seeing each other.

'I'm so sad that our affair has had to come to an end,' she wrote. 'But I'm happy you've found someone who will make you happy, who you can make a life with.'

That was good, he'd told her about me ...

But then it went on ... 'It was really embarrassing when I had to go to the VD clinic ...'

The truth dawned. So much for 'waiting for the right time' and all that crap.

'I was very disappointed with you, that you had done this to me, but there is nothing we can do about that now,' she wrote, 'and I wish you well. I will miss you darling ...'

I picked Rick up and he was full of the joys of spring — and himself.

'I won! You can drive because I've had a bit to drink.'

'OK, well you can hold this then,' I said and passed him the letter.

His face went into a kind of grimace.

'Aaaah!' he said. 'Yes, um, I was going to tell you about that but I didn't quite know how to.'

'So it was obviously all lies then, all that stuff about how you wanted to wait before we made love, how I was special.' I was hurt. More than that, I was furious.

'Well how am I meant to say to you: "Look, I can't sleep with you darlin' because I've got VD!" So I had to say something ... and I meant what I said.'

'Yes, but what about "I want it to be the right time, I want you to be the right one and I don't want to mess you up and everything!"'

'Well, if I had told you the truth it would have messed you up, wouldn't it? And I would have lost you, wouldn't I? I don't want to be on my own. And I don't want to lose you ...'

And so he talked his way out of it, swearing that he'd never see Janet again (which, of course, he did soon afterwards). But I forgave him. I wanted to believe him and when he made love to me that night he was so loving and gentle I knew he really cared for me. I was the one he was engaged to, I was the one he was going to marry. The main obstacle stopping us getting married was that we had nowhere to live and Rick didn't want to leave Woking for somewhere cheaper. He'll always live in, or near, Woking. He feels safe there.

I didn't mind waiting. I knew we'd get married one day and we were very young. Rick dreamed of stardom as a rock star and I had my dreams too; I wanted to be a photographer. I had left my job at Efco to work in a photographer's studio in Woking High Street. It was great, and the photographer I

Patty Parfitt

worked for was teaching me the business. To begin with, I was doing all the menial jobs, but the boss lent me his Nikon to experiment with some shots, and the plan was that I'd go to Tech in the evenings to study and work my way up.

Of course, that didn't go down well with Rick. He wanted me available whenever he wanted to see me — he hasn't changed much in that respect. He used to pick me up in the Jag for lunch but he was always late bringing me back.

The first and second times it happened I got a real telling off. The third time I was told that if I was late again I'd get the sack.

'Oh fuck 'em,' said Rick. 'Leave the place.' So, stupidly, I did, I went on the dole and instead of collecting me for lunch Rick used to drive me to the Labour Exchange to get my money. Then my brother opened a boutique and I went to work there. Rick liked that — it was much more fitting, he said, for the girlfriend of a rock star! And, he added, that since my sister-in-law would be working with me I wouldn't be able to chat up any men who came in!

Looking back, of course, I should have hung on at the photographer's but I was very young, crazy about Rick and he was the centre of my world. We both wanted to have some fun before we settled down. Besides there was the band. That was the number one priority. I totally understood this.

The gigs were going well and the fans, at least most of them, seemed to like the new rock set. Quo were very much the people's band. I went along in The Min to lots of gigs or, while the band were playing, I'd go round to Nuff and Pat's. That was Alan Lancaster's nickname — Nuff. When girls would say: 'Why Nuff?' He'd say: 'Because I'm big enough!' Alan, apparently, is well-endowed, not that I would know.

Rick had his own line for the girls too — and he hasn't changed it in thirty years. He says: 'Hi, I'm Dick — do you like it?'

Laughing All Over The World

Francis has always been nicknamed Frame because he used to work in an opticians, and Rick was called Tricky for obvious reasons. Francis also calls him Dick. What I think he means is Dick-head!

The band were finding their feet and working on their new style, and we travelled to gigs all over the place. A favourite was The Marquee in Wardour Street where Quo played with many big names. It's hard now to describe the atmosphere of those times.

Many bands were in the same position as Quo, struggling for their break. In those days Rick and Francis were really good mates, too, they met up when the band weren't playing even though Francis lived miles away from Woking, in Dulwich, and they'd always ring each other up before a gig to find out what the other one was wearing — they always wanted to dress roughly the same.

But Rick didn't like me talking to members of other bands. If he saw me talking to someone while he was on stage he'd look daggers at me and say afterwards: 'Don't you realise they're only talking to you because you're with me? I don't want you talking to them because you don't realise how dangerous it can be.' I think he was always worried I'd go off with one of them, which I never would have, I was too crazy about him.

We often used to see Thin Lizzy at the gigs. They'd do half an hour or so before Quo went on and their lead singer, the black Irishman Phil Lynott, was a lovely man, a real charmer with an incredible voice. He sadly died of a drug overdose in 1986 and he kept ringing me in the days before he died. He wanted company, but one of my greatest regrets is that I couldn't go because I had my parents staying with me. I never saw any signs that he was stoned at the gigs, I wasn't really aware of drugs then – but he did like a drink, and he was my drinking partner and would sometimes sit with me watching

Patty Parfitt

while Quo played. He had a wonderful sense of humour and Quo had a lot of respect for him as a musician — he and Rick wrote some beautiful songs together which have never been recorded but really should be — and for Thin Lizzy, about the only other band around then that they did respect, although they thought they were a bit deep — one thing Quo have never been is deep!

In front of everyone, Quo and Thin Lizzy were best mates. But behind closed doors it didn't stop Quo making racist jokes about Phil.

Rick didn't like me talking to Phil, but Phil obviously liked me and I liked him too. That sexy voice. So, when Rick started to really kick up about it I had to make excuses to Phil not to sit with him.

Quite often all the other girls didn't go to the gigs and I'd go on my own or with Linda, Spud's girlfriend. Pat, Alan's wife, came along occasionally too.

One night I was late for a gig and arrived at The Toby Jug when the band were already on stage. As I was parking my dad's old 1100 I saw Steve, one of the roadies, come out of the stage door and get into the back of the van they used for carrying all the equipment.

I went to the stage door but it seemed to be locked. I couldn't get in so I called out: 'Steve!' He obviously hadn't heard me so I went over to the van and opened the back door. And there was Steve helping himself to Nuff's wife, Pat, in the back of the van! I didn't know whether they'd seen me or not, they were obviously very engrossed, so I went around to the front of the pub thinking: 'Oh shit, shit, shit — what am I going to do?'

I went in and watched the band and Pat came in just as they were finishing.

She came over smiling.

'Are you all right?'

I was flustered and very embarrassed. Don't forget, I was only eighteen.

'Yeah, I'm fine.'

'Oh good,' she said. 'Were you working late?'

'Well, my dad was and I couldn't get the car so that's why I'm a bit late. I'm sorry if I ... er ...'

'Oh, let's not mention it. You *won't* mention it, will you?'

'No, of course not.'

'Let's forget it,' said Pat. I couldn't agree fast enough!

Only last year I found out that Alan had known all along that she was screwing around. I got a fair idea as time went on, because when Alan and Pat had their baby Alan (he now has two children of his own!), she didn't go to so many gigs and sometimes, instead of watching the band, I'd go round to her place until the band came home.

We'd have a take-away and a good natter. She liked me but she absolutely adored Rick and I'm sure she'd had him too. Sometimes, when Rick dropped me off at Pat and Nuff's, I'd go in to find that she was ready to go out. As soon as Rick disappeared around the corner she'd say: 'I've got to go out for an hour or so, you'll look after little Alan, won't you?' Off she went, usually with Steve.

Once he rang up and asked for her and I had to say she'd gone out.

'Oh,' he said sounding awkward. 'I just had something that I had to bring round.'

'Aren't you working tonight then?'

'Er ... no ... I'm off tonight ... Er, I'd better go.'

Pat used to reappear about fifteen minutes before the boys got back from the gig, by which time I was usually pacing the floor worrying whether she'd make it in time.

Then she'd sit down, they'd turn up and Alan would say, 'Hello darlin', hello Patty. You two had a good time?'

'Oh yes,' Pat would grin. 'We've had a great time, haven't we?'

Patty Parfitt

It wasn't exactly a love match but, like the rest of the band, Alan wasn't always squeaky clean himself. He used to go off with groupies occasionally. You'd see them waiting at the bar before the gig and the band would saunter over and chat to them, sizing them up, before deciding which one to invite backstage after the gig. You could always spot who had been chosen, too, because the boys couldn't resist showing off and hip-wiggling during the gig in the general direction of the girl they'd chosen. Then the girl would go backstage for a drink and maybe a smoke and the boys would say: 'We can't go to my place — we'll go to yours,' and off they went. Sometimes it wasn't even that complicated; they just headed for the nearest loo and did it there. You could never get into the loo — there was always someone in there banging away and someone else, a roadie, guarding the door.

The groupies had no shame about chatting up the boys and making clear just what it was they wanted. Spud was a shocker — he went with dozens of them. He'd go with anything, he wasn't fussy, but he preferred them young.

Sometimes the groupies got passed around from band to band. One might sleep with Amen Corner, and then when they'd all had her, they'd say to The Move, another band: 'We've finished with her — you have her.' For the groupies, the best thing was to have the lead singer. They might sleep with the road crew first, then management, then the band, starting with the drummer (which wasn't very prestigious apparently) and banging their way up to the lead singer.

Rock bands are sexy and most of them could pick and choose who they went with. Even chaps who weren't gorgeous could get girls.

I've no idea how many groupies Rick has slept with — quite a few I should think. After all, he's been pulling them since he was a teenager at the holiday camps, but I think, at least I hope, that for the first year or so we were together he was faithful to me.

Gradually the band's hard work and dedication began to pay off. People were beginning to take notice and I noticed a subtle change in them, too, especially Rick.

He was drinking more — they all were — and they were smoking much more marijuana. Backstage the air was thick with it. It was all part of the rock 'n' roll lifestyle. Then, suddenly, he said he didn't want to get married. With the money coming in, he wanted to taste a bit more of this life, and he didn't want to be tied down with a wife and maybe a family. I was very hurt and upset but I said I understood — I just wanted to stay with him.

But then he really started to change. Ricky, my Ricky, became Rick Parfitt. The others changed, too, but never as much as Rick did. He became really big-headed and used to show off to me in front of people, which he'd never done before. He'd say things to strangers like: 'Don't you know who I am?' and I'd get really embarrassed.

It made me cringe. At last, the band were starting to get good, encouraging publicity and Rick, for one, was starting to believe it. Rick loved it. He was like a little boy, trying to act cool and loving all the attention. In a way it was funny, but at the same time I was scared. I felt I was losing him.

The band were very much in a party mood. They began to drink constantly and were pissed a lot of the time. Before, they couldn't afford spirits so they usually stuck to beer, but now they drank dark rum, brandies and also whisky which makes Rick more aggressive. It's when he's drunk whisky that he starts smashing up rooms or chucking dining room suites in swimming pools.

The downside of this blossoming success — and it wasn't even big time yet — was that Rick became much more selfish. He lapped up all the attention and he didn't seem to need me

Patty Parfitt

around as much as he had before.

It wasn't nearly so much fun. What with the booze, dope and shouting out of car windows: 'Wahey! Bet you don't know who I am!' at one o'clock in the morning in Woking High Street, it was beginning to get a bit embarrassing. Of course, I still loved him to bits but he wasn't as loving or as appreciative as he had been before.

I was always having to carry him out of pubs and clubs, pissed after the gig, and then he'd fall down in the road and I'd be there in my platforms trying to lift him up and get him into The Min. The others weren't quite so bad. Alan just got a bit tipsy and Francis was usually smoking dope so he was off the planet but in a quiet sort of way. But Rick was usually roaring drunk and he didn't care what he did, he was enjoying himself.

The crunch came when they were recording *On the Level*, their last album for Pye at their studios behind London's Marble Arch. Rick wanted me there for the recording and told me to bring my Dad's car up so I could drive him home.

I watched the recording and then he remembered that the record company had ordered him a car home. He couldn't cancel it, he said, because that would have been impolite.

'But what about me?'

'Oh, you'll just have to follow us.'

'Cancel the bloody car!'

'I can't do that. The guy's been waiting for ages already.'

So I dutifully followed and his car dropped him off at home. I was just parking when Rick said: 'I've run out of fags — can you just pop down the road and get me some?'

And with that he went indoors and shut the door. So off I went, like a mug, down to the cigarette machine in the High Street. It was one in the morning. I was tired. I'd had a few drinks — and I forgot to turn my lights on.

The police car spotted me immediately. I was breathalysed,

and then taken to the police station where they let me make one phone call. I rang Rick.

'I'm at the police station ...'

'Oh, don't fuck around Patty,' he said. Admittedly I did used to play the fool sometimes.

'Honestly, I've been done for drunk driving ...'

'It's not funny, Patty. I'm tired. If you can't bring the fags around then don't bother.' And he hung up.

The policemen looked at me sympathetically and allowed me another call. I rang Dad and told him that I was in Woking jail. Poor old Dad got up and came to bail me out.

Rick came round the next day, just a little sheepish.

'I'm sorry, I thought you were mucking about. But what could I have done? I'd had too much to drink ... I didn't have a car anyway ... and I was tired.'

Then I didn't see him for a few days and, for some strange reason, things were different after that. We didn't argue or row — we never had — but I wouldn't see him for days at a time.

He always said: 'I'll see you soon.'

'When?'

'I don't know, Patty, I've got a lot of things on and the band is getting better all the time. You know I've got a lot of writing to do and I can't do that with you around.' In fact, I'd rarely seen him write a song but I accepted it meekly. Until I found out he was seeing Janet again, she of the VD clinic. Alan told me. I should have guessed the day the band turned up in their Bentley outside his Mum and Dad's.

To celebrate their burgeoning success they'd jointly bought this fab car and they wanted to ride to the gig in it. They all took turns to have it a day at a time and this day was Alan's turn so he drove with Francis and John to pick up Rick from my place. Rick was dead chuffed — the neighbours were dead impressed, too.

Once it had been admired, the band came into the house

Patty Parfitt

for a cuppa.

'What do you want me to do?' I asked Rick. He'd already said he didn't want me to go to the gig. 'Don't come to this gig because it's not a great gig,' he'd said. It was a big student gig and some of those weren't much fun.

He looked a bit awkward. 'Look, we're leaving early because we want to go and have a drink before we go on ... I might ring you afterwards, and then you can come round, you know.'

What he meant was that I could come round and sleep with him at his place. We couldn't sleep together at my house unless Mum and Dad went out but his Mum and Dad didn't mind if I slept with him there.

'OK,' I said.

Rick and Francis went out to the Bentley, and I followed with Alan. As we got to the front door Alan turned to me. He was always very sweet to me.

'Look Patty,' he said. 'I can't let you go through this. I just want to tell you, and I know I shouldn't, but he's still seeing Janet. That's where he's going now and we're picking him up later. He's lying to you. I don't know why he's doing it and I'm sorry ...'

I couldn't speak. I felt as if someone had kicked me in the stomach. I went upstairs to my bedroom and cried all night. Rick didn't phone for about three days.

'Are you coming round then?' he said.

'OK. I think we need to talk.'

There was a pause. 'OK. Can we go out for a drink? Come around about 1.00pm.'

He didn't know that I knew he'd been seeing Janet, but he sounded uneasy, and to add insult to injury, I had to borrow my dad's 1100 to go round to Rick's because he'd lent The Min to her!

'Look, I'm sorry,' he said on the telephone. 'But Janet is in dire straits. She smashed her Ventura driving back to West Byfleet. Alex is away on business and she's too scared to tell him she's smashed the car. She can't hire one because he'd get the bill and find out ...' he spluttered on. 'So, anyway, I told her she could borrow Min.'

Considering Janet was my fiancé's mistress, I thought this was a bit rich but I just murmured OK and said I'd see him at one. But I couldn't wait to talk to him. I decided to go around early. I knew his mum came home from work at one for lunch and I didn't want to talk to him in front of her, so I arrived at midday.

The door was open, so I walked in as I always did. I could see Rick and Janet standing there in the front room, their arms around each other, kissing, engrossed in each other, holding each other tightly.

They obviously hadn't heard me, but I wasn't going to run away so I made a noise and they jumped apart. 'Oh, hello,' he said, 'Janet has just brought these things around for Mum and she's, er, brought the car back and we were just, er, saying goodbye ...'

Janet looked completely unfazed by the situation. She smiled like a Cheshire cat.

'So, *you're* Patty. Oh you're gorgeous, so much more pretty and more beautiful than Rick described.'

I didn't know what to say but managed to mumble: 'Oh, that's nice.'

With hindsight I can see she was being really bitchy, especially as she went on: 'I'm so glad, you're so suited to each other. I'm just saying goodbye to my little boy! By the way, thanks very much for letting me borrow the car.'

'That's fine,' I said. 'I'll go and wait outside.'

She grinned that grin. 'Oh, you don't have to do that.'

'I'd rather,' I said and snivelled out.

I thought they'd come out straight away but it was another

Patty Parfitt

five minutes or so before they joined me outside the front door. She got in her Vauxhall Ventura (which didn't have a mark on it) and drove off.

Then Rick said: 'Come on then, let's go to the pub. Look, I had to help Janet out. It was a bit emotional when you came in, unfortunately you arrived at the wrong time and,' he looked accusingly at me, 'I did tell you one o'clock.'

'I didn't want to upset your Mum. I didn't want to talk in front of her.'

'You didn't come around spying on me then? You wouldn't do that, would you? D'you know, you are the nicest person that I've ever met ...'

I was melting again. 'I came round early so we could talk privately.'

I couldn't say that Alan had told me about Janet — that would have ruined the atmosphere within the band and, after all, it was the number one priority. Besides I didn't want Alan to be hurt. So I said: 'It's just that a couple of people have seen you out with Janet ... and you were kissing her just now ...'

'I'm really sorry,' he said. 'But, look, this is definitely it. I don't want to see her any more. I only want you, Patty.'

It was what I wanted to hear. 'Good,' I said. 'Can we go back to normal now?'

'Yes, of course,' he said and gave me a cuddle. 'But you've got to understand that I've got a lot on at the moment so I won't be able to see you as much as before. The band is really picking up now. Anyway, have I told you about ...' and, typically, Rick changed the subject. I knew that Janet had been discussed and I wasn't supposed to mention it again.

Everything was fine for a couple of weeks then it was the same story. He'd ring — then he wouldn't. He'd turn up — and then he wouldn't.

'Are you doing any gigs?' I'd ask.

Laughing All Over The World

'No.'

'Are you and Frame writing then?'

'No, I'm not really writing ...'

While I was hanging around waiting for Rick, my brother was getting fed up with me only turning up for work occasionally at the boutique.

He said he couldn't pay me a week's wages when I wasn't turning up for the whole week which was fair enough because he did have a business to run.

Things were really picking up now for Quo, and Rick was getting more and more distant. It was Francis who had a word with me in the end. He said he couldn't stand seeing me making a fool of myself. Francis is a strange man but at times he can be very kind and a very good friend.

One night, after a gig, he and I found ourselves alone and he started talking.

'Be careful, Patty,' he said. 'The fame's going to Rick's head and it's only just started. The money's beginning to come in and he's changing. We all are, I suppose ...'

I wasn't quite sure what he was trying to tell me.

'He's doing things he never used to do before and you're going to get hurt ...'

'What do you mean? He hasn't got VD again, has he?'

'Oh no ... but he probably will the way he's going ...'

'So ... he's seeing other girls?'

'That's a polite way of putting it. He's changing. Be careful or you're going to get very hurt.' I always listened to Francis, everybody did, because he's not a talkative person so when he wants to tell you something you pay attention.

Looking back I was a fool. I still went to the gigs even though sometimes I knew that Rick would be going off with someone else afterwards. But I was hoping and praying that he'd get over all this and things would be as they were before.

Francis was sweet. He'd always come over to pay me some

Patty Parfitt

attention and he started coming on to me saying: 'Oh come on, Patty. You drop me home, you know he's going off with someone else ...'

It was difficult, and really upsetting. Rick hadn't finished with me but he was just keeping me dangling on a thread. One night I took two of my old workmates to The Marquee — and Rick invited one of his Mum's closest friends, another Lily.

I'd already heard on the grapevine that she was one of Rick's latest but he laughed it off: 'Oh, you're just getting it all out of proportion. She's going through a bad time, she's just getting divorced and I go around there now and then and watch telly with her. Sometimes I buy her a drink or take her out to dinner.' That last bit really irritated me — Rick never took me out. I used to have to buy my own meals unless Frame or Alan came up with the money.

So I arrived at the venue with my friends and there was Jean Rossi waiting for me outside.

'Patty, don't come in — Rick's brought this bloody old woman.'

Jean was getting agitated but I wasn't having any of it.

'Look, I'm going in. I've brought my friends all this bloody way and I'm going in ...'

'Francis and I were going to have a word with you afterwards anyway.' Jean was embarrassed. 'We've talked about it and we wanted to tell you what's been happening because it's really not fair. We think a lot of you, you know.' I knew they did.

Jean and Francis were always good to me. I used to babysit with Jean quite often, while Quo played gigs and Francis and Jean invited me to their house a lot. They knew Rick was messing up and they wanted to make sure I was all right, although I'm not sure what was on Francis' mind. It was that look on his face. I'd seen that look before!

I knew Rick and I were nearing the end and this was an

Laughing All Over The World

excruciatingly embarrassing situation, but there was no way I was going to quit now, so we all went in.

I knew Janet was older — well, late thirties anyway — but this woman was *much* older. I was stunned. Rick was friendly but distant. To his new lover he was very friendly and very close. He took her home after the gig and wasn't heard of again for two nights.

It was the last straw. Fuck him — I decided to go to Australia! I knew I had to get away from Rick — he was ruling my life and he didn't even want me. And in those days the Australian government were offering trips to Australia for just £10.

You could come home whenever you wanted, but if you returned to the UK before the end of two years you had to pay your fares both ways — after two years you just paid your fare back.

I went to two more gigs to see Rick, and Frame announced on stage that I was going to Australia at the end of the week. Rick, of course, refused to believe it. He just told me not to be so stupid.

Then he said: 'You won't be there for long. I've got to do my thing and you've got to do yours, but when I phone you'll come back.'

On the way back from that last gig (Rick had already left with someone else) we played this mad game with all of us driving the car — Francis worked the brake, Bob had his leg over the seat working the clutch, and I did the indicators and looked out of the window to see where we were going. It was a laugh and miraculously we made it to Dulwich in one piece. We dropped Bob off and drove on to Francis' place. He told me that Jean was probably asleep so asked me to park up around the back of the garage.

'Look Patty,' he said, 'you've got to go off and be independent and maybe then he'll get his head together. He's

Patty Parfitt

a real bastard, you know. Even I don't like him any more and not many people do now. He's turned into some kind of fucking monster and we don't like the birds he's with. With all the warnings you've had you've held on for a damn sight longer than we thought you would. Go on, go off and enjoy yourself and then come back only if he's a decent person to come back to. I'll let you know.'

Then he put his arm around me: 'Come on then, give us a cuddle.'

I burst into tears. 'Why did it all go wrong, Francis? Why did it all go wrong?'

'It's all right, darlin',' he said softly and his other arm went round my shoulders. 'It's all right.' And then we were snogging passionately.

I pushed him away when I realised that we were both getting excited.

'No, I can't have this. I like Jean too much ...'

'So do I,' he said. 'But we're not going to see you for two years ... it's not going to hurt anyone ...' and we kissed again. I tried to push him away.

'This is too much,' I whispered between kisses, 'this has got to stop before it starts ...' and after another long, deep kiss I pushed him away from me, we said goodbye and he finally got out of the car. I drove home in tears.

I saw Rick the next day and we went to Clapham Common for a kiss and a cuddle and played our favourite eight-track, 'After the Gold Rush' by Neil Young. I cried a lot.

'I'll see you tomorrow,' he said.

'But I'm going tomorrow!' I cried.

'Oh, yeah,' he said absently. 'That's right.'

The next day I flew to Australia. I knew no one there, I wasn't yet 21 — my birthday was in two weeks time — and I kept telling myself that it was going to be a big adventure but inside I just felt wretched and miserable.

The day I left, Rick came round to my house to return a jacket I'd left in his car the night before. My brother-in-law answered the door.

'Is she here?' said Rick.

'No, she's gone.'

'Oh, what time is she coming back then?'

'No Rick, she's *gone*, gone to Australia.'

'Really? ... She's really left?'

'She left half an hour ago, the jacket'll have to stay here.'

Rick's mum told me years later that Rick went home and cried his eyes out. The following day he went round to see my Mum and Dad and said he was sorry. But they knew I was angry with him and told him that it was his fault I'd left. But he kept going around there, expecting me to come back.

At the end of that week he phoned me.

'I honestly didn't think you were going to go,' he said.

'Well, I'm here.'

'Love, come home. I want you to come home.'

'No. I've got to stay.'

'If you don't come home I'll go and marry someone else,' he said sulkily.

'If you feel you've got to, then do it,' I said, 'because if you really wanted me you'd wait the year or two that I'm away. I'm not coming back after just one week.'

We said goodbye with him promising to ring again soon.

Seven months later he married someone else.

4

Down, Down, Deeper and Down Under

I had only been in Australia a month or so, and I was feeling low, but from home I got continual news of the Quo. They were going from strength to strength, building up a good fan base, and then I heard that Colin Johnson, their manager, had decided that after their success in Britain, it was time to hit Europe, especially France and Germany.

In the end, they got ten gold albums out of France and they also made it big in Germany. The gigs went down well — but Rick was often lonely. He hated the empty hotel room with no female company. So he hit on an excellent idea and sent a roadie out to buy a shapely shop mannequin — complete with blonde wig. He called her Danielle and went shopping for her clothes — designer clothes — and underwear himself.

On arrival at a hotel a roadie would assemble and dress her. She was sat on a chair and there she waited for Rick until he came back from the gig. She was almost the perfect woman — she looked good, did as she was told,

Patty Parfitt

and she didn't answer back!

But what happened between them once the bedroom door was shut no one knew — or liked to imagine!

One night the band had a night off gigging and they went off to a nightclub to get smashed. Rick was angry and he felt lonely and miserable.

'The first girl who comes through that door I'll marry,' he said. 'I just hope she's not a dog!'

'Yeah, right, Rick,' said Francis.

The door opened and in walked a cracker — a brunette, classy, very much a lady.

The others didn't do too badly but it was Alan Lancaster who pulled her and at closing time she invited them all back to her flat for a smoke. They didn't need asking twice but once there Rick moved in and swiftly elbowed Alan out. Alan was four inches too short for her anyway, and so stoned he hardly noticed what Rick had done. Soon she and Rick had eyes and hands only for each other. Rick was smitten — this girl was something else. In front of the others he said: 'I'm going to marry you.'

Her name was Marietta.

*   *   *

After their success in Britain and Europe it was time to conquer continents new, so Quo headed off to my neck of the woods — Australia. They weren't topping the bill, but were supporting Noddy Holder's Slade and the band Caravan. It was a foot in the door and the boys were looking forward to it — even laid-back Frame.

They arrived in January at the height of the Australian summer, and Spud managed to pull even before he'd staggered drunkenly off the plane. She was a stunning brunette air hostess, and even better, she had agreed to meet him back at the hotel later. Spud had broken up with Linda before I left for Australia.

Spud pleaded with the others: 'Please, please don't screw this up for me. She's really cool, man, I really like her.'

Rick and Francis reassured him.

'Don't worry, man. Good luck.'

Spud bought her drinks, chatted away, and finally, feeling optimistic, led her up to his room. Once upstairs they kissed passionately, he tore back the sheets — and there was an inflatable doll, fully blown up, mouth and legs open ready for action.

'You bastard!' shrieked the air hostess and stormed out.

'You bastards!' shouted Spud, and the others fell out of the walk-in wardrobe screaming with hysterical laughter.

Doris the Doll subsequently accompanied Quo across Australia. Pass-the-Doris became a favourite game on the Quo tour bus.

Although I was furious with Rick when I left the UK, when I learned they were touring in Australia, I was really excited. Rick was always in the back of my mind — it had always seemed inconceivable that I would never see him again.

When he phoned, I was a bit thrown. I missed him desperately. But he still thought I didn't mean I was *going* to Australia even though I was *in* Australia.

'You'll be back, you'll be back,' he said. 'But,' he added generously, 'have a nice time, have a nice holiday and I'll see you soon.'

That was the last time I spoke to him for a while and, although he was always in my thoughts, I knew I had to get on with the business of carving out a life for myself in Oz if I was going to survive — otherwise I'd be scuttling home with my tail between my legs and that would have been too much to bear.

I needed some time alone. I had to grow up in my own way, without Rick there shaping me, telling me what to say or do. I had to be my own person. Besides, I always knew deep in my heart that Rick and I would be together, be married and have a child one day. He knew it, too.

Patty Parfitt

The last time we were alone together he said: 'We both know we're going to be together one day, we'll get married, we'll do the whole lot. If it's not in two years or ten years, it'll be in fifteen years or twenty years and we'll be back together for keeps. You know that.'

I said: 'I know, that's why I'm going away.'

Typically he then changed tack. 'OK. But anyway you'll be back in a couple of months,' and he gave me a kiss for luck. It didn't really matter how many years it was going to take, we knew that in some way we'd always be together. As it turned out, we were right. We still are joined today, we have our son Harry, so it's for ever.

Meanwhile, I had to get myself together in Australia. I scoured the papers looking for jobs and somewhere to live. Finally, I found a shared place in Bondi — not as wonderful as it sounds!

But the three girls I was to share with were really nice, especially one called Kim who became my best friend, and I soon got some temping jobs. I talked to Kim about Rick, of course, but, although she'd heard of Quo and 'Pictures of Matchstick Men' vaguely, she'd never heard of him! So life settled down into some kind of routine. I loved Australia and Sydney and the easy-going life — and the oysters!

Even so, I missed Rick like mad. After a few months I got a letter. For him to write at all was a miracle and the fact that it reached me was pretty amazing too — the envelope was addressed upside down and Sydney spelled Sidney! Rick told me later it was the first time he'd ever written to a girl — and the last! I kept it for years, until my bag was stolen only a few years ago and I lost it. I couldn't have cared less about losing the bag and my cash, but that letter meant a lot to me.

Romantic, however, it was not. Most of it was about cars — the one he'd had which he'd smashed up and the new one he'd bought to replace it. 'You'll love it. I won't tell you what it is but it's got ... well, the suspenders have been let down ... can't spell suspenders (I think he meant suspension!) ... and it's got a stripe down the side. You guessed it! It's a right fast bubble car! No! No! Actually it's a Capri, a tasty Capri! I bet your (sic) grinning now!' I was! There was a little PS. 'I really miss you and I didn't think I'd miss you as much as I did and still do, so when you get this letter can you phone me?'

Of course I rang. It was the same story. Rick wanted me to come home but I said I was staying for at least a year. 'You'll be touring, you've got new records coming out and everything and it will be good for both of us.'

'Well, we'll see. I can't just sit and wait forever but all right, stay just a bit longer. Give me another ring in a month or so.'

He rarely rang me — it was always me who had to ring him — and if I left it too long he'd say: 'Why haven't you rung? Got a new boyfriend?'

It cost me an absolute fortune and I could ill afford it.

The next thing I heard was that he was going out with a German girl and he might get married. My mum got all the news and gossip about Rick from his parents and passed it on to me. She wrote in high dudgeon: 'Rick is seeing this German girl and there's talk they're going to get MARRIED!'

Strangely, although I realised this was probably serious, I wasn't that bothered. I still knew deep down that Rick and I would be together one day, whatever happened in the interim. The only problem was that, as far as I was concerned, it put me off anyone else. I wanted to have fun, I wanted to see and learn a bit about the world, to live a little but I didn't want a serious relationship — my heart belonged to Rick. It still does, I suppose. I can't help that.

The band were touring in Australia in January and as time went on, I got more and more excited. I'd missed them all.

At last, the great day came. I met them at Sydney airport and it was kisses and cuddles all round. Rick's not a romantic man, but he at least admitted he was pleased to see me. Then it was straight back to the hotel for a press conference. It was Quo's first tour of Australia and it was important that they made a success of it. Slade were topping the bill and getting

Patty Parfitt

most of the attention, Lindisfarne and Caravan were on the same tour, too. Even so, it was a great opportunity for Quo to make their mark in Australia.

I was looking good and Rick noticed instantly — he always clocks what a woman's wearing — and he liked the mini skirt. It was also a perfect opportunity to show off my Aussie tan.

Kim and her boyfriend had given me a lift to the airport but Rick didn't like that at all.

'What's that bloke doing around you all the time?' he hissed at the press conference.

'He's Kim's boyfriend.'

'I don't like him.'

At the press conference, when everyone was having drinks, Francis took me aside. I blushed when I thought of our last meeting and the snogs in the car, especially when he looked me up and down and told me that I looked good. He steered me into a quiet corner of the room, out of earshot of all the journalists and Rick.

'Look, Patty,' said Francis. 'If you don't get your act together and get your arse back home he's going to marry this German girl, Marietta.'

'Well,' I said hesitantly. 'If that's what he wants to do. He's blackmailing me, Francis, isn't he? I can't leave here yet. Not until I've been here a year.'

'Look, you know you two are going to get married eventually so why not come back now?' Then he shrugged. 'Well, it's up to you. I'm just telling you.'

I gave him a kiss on the cheek. I was, and still am, very fond of Francis. He and Jean used to write to me regularly when I was first out in Australia (well, Jean wrote and Frame added a line or two!) and I always appreciated that.

Then he went on to tell me that Marietta came from a very rich family. He said she was educated, that she'd been to university and she spoke five different languages.

From all that Francis said I could see that this relationship, unlike the dozens of others, was serious and I knew the way

Rick's mind was working. He was 26, everyone else in the band was married (even if they did play around) and he didn't want to be on his own. He liked the idea of someone to come home to, that's what he'd been used to. He was still living at home with his Mum and Dad and he'd had enough of it.

'I'm not going to be blackmailed into going back, I'm not,' I said to Francis firmly and, ever since, I've wondered if I made a mistake. But I was having a great time, I was independent and I didn't want to give it all up for boring England. So I thought: 'No, I'll make him wait. I'll stay here just a little longer.'

The tour of Australia didn't last long, just two weeks. They came back to Sydney to do their last gig and I stayed with Rick at the hotel for a couple of nights. It was magic but we always ended up arguing about me coming home.

'Apparently, if I don't come back you'll marry this German girl, then,' I said.

'I don't know,' said Rick. 'Of course I've been seeing her but what do you expect? You've been away for a long time. You've probably been with someone else, too.'

'No, I haven't. But what you do … that's fine.'

It was so odd. I *knew* I was going to marry him one day so I didn't feel jealous about Marietta, not at all.

But, of course, I wanted to know all about her. I heard that she'd gone blonde after meeting Rick — all his women are blondes. She'd also slimmed down — another Rick side-effect. Put on a bit of weight and he doesn't like it at all. He grabs hold of the fat on your hips and pinches and says: 'Ugh, handles. They'll have to go.' And then you starve yourself until you meet approval.

I couldn't resist dropping a few rude references to Germany into the conversation plus things I'd heard from Mum, Rick's Cousin Sue and Jean Rossi.

'How did you know about that? Did Francis tell you?'

'Ermmm,' I'd say mysteriously.

'Well, I don't know how Francis knows anything anyway.

Patty Parfitt

She lives in Germany and, well, that's it.' Then he'd reach for me again and say: 'You'd better get your skates on, you know, or you'll miss out.'

'I think I will.'

'Well, I'll give you a month to think about it. I'll ring you.'

The boys enjoyed Australia even though it was a fleeting visit. They also had their fair share of groupies, even Rick, although he had me.

But most important of all was that Alan Lancaster fell bang in love with a smashing girl called Dayle. She was there on the very first day at the press conference, invited by a friend of hers who was a journalist. She was only 17 at the time and, after she and Alan were introduced, he came over to me with eyes like saucers and said: 'Wow! I like her, I mean I *really* like her.'

'She's nice,' I said. 'But somehow I don't think that Pat will like her very much.'

He looked at me sadly.

'Oh come on, Patty, you know about Pat and me, it doesn't really matter.'

That was the first inkling I had that Alan knew that Pat had been playing around. I had my suspicions about Rick and her, too. She once told me that Rick had shown her the blue velvet suit he bought for our 'wedding', he showed it to me. I used to wonder before, 'So, when was that then exactly?'

'What do you think of Dayle, Patty?' asked Alan.

'I think she's really nice, but she's also very young. Don't hurt her, you mustn't do that.'

'I won't. Honestly.'

In fact, where women were concerned, Alan was much better than the others. Of course he was no angel, and he went off with the odd groupie or two, but he was much more sensitive, and nicer than Francis, Spud and, I'm afraid, Rick.

I'd met Dayle before, and the next day she rang to ask me out to lunch. She wanted to know all about Alan.

It wasn't an easy lunch to begin with because I liked Dayle

and I really thought she had to know about Pat. In the end I just blurted it out: 'Look, I've got to tell you — I can't hold this in. He's married.'

'I know. He rang me this morning and told me. I just wanted to know if you'd tell me.'

'I had to — you're too nice.' I was getting wiser and I also knew the band too well. And that was the beginning of a long-lasting friendship between Dayle and I.

I rang Alan.

'I've had lunch with Dayle, Alan. You can't hurt her. Don't go out with her.'

'Too late,' he said. 'I've absolutely fallen head over heels for her. It's incredible. It's like you and Rick years ago.'

For a few years Dayle travelled backwards and forwards to England to see him and, in the end they married and, I'm happy to say, have lived happily ever after.

While Alan was busy being smitten with Dayle the rest of the band were dedicated to enjoying Australia.

The drinking had increased enormously. They were still drinking brandy and Coke but now they were very large brandies with just a dash of Coke. They were still into dope, especially Francis, but Alan and Rick had progressed to taking a bit of speed and popping pills as well to keep them going.

Everyone around them was out of it most of the time but there was an unspoken rule that they wouldn't really go for it until after they'd played on stage. Then all the brakes were off. Later that rule slipped and a few times they appeared on stage so far off the planet that they simply couldn't perform.

As quickly as they arrived they were gone. It was a whirlwind visit that left me feeling dazed. Rick was wasted a lot of the time. I'd go out with him and then crawl home at 3.00am to grab a couple of hours sleep before I started work.

Then I'd go back to him at teatime and the whole thing would start all over again. It was fun but totally exhausting. I felt all kinds of mixed emotions as I said goodbye to Rick at the hotel. I didn't go to the airport with them because I

Patty Parfitt

couldn't afford the taxi back — and no taxi fare was on offer. As usual, when I was out with Rick in those days, I'd spent a fortune.

Rick and I chatted as they prepared to go.

'Oh, did I tell you? Janet's had her boobs done! They're really great!' Thanks Rick!

He kissed me hard.

'I'll call you. See you in a month.'

He just refused to accept that I wasn't going straight back to the UK and him. 'Don't forget I love you,' he said, 'I'll marry whoever if you don't come home. I really need to move out of Mum and Dad's. I can't stand it any more. I want you to come back because I need you. Stop being indecisive. Make your mind up.'

And then he was gone.

True to his word he rang a month later, drunk at the time.

'You're not coming are you?' he said, sounding annoyed.

'No.'

'I knew you weren't. Well, when you do come home I might see you and I might not.'

'Look, it's only for a couple of months, then I'll have been here for a year and I don't have to pay my fare out as well as my fare back.'

'But I want you back *now*.' After a few more curt words he hung up.

I was distraught. I really wasn't sure whether I'd made the right decision. But, if I went back, would things really be different? It didn't feel like the right time to get married to Rick or anyone else.

If we did marry, I was afraid it wouldn't work. And I was right — he wasn't ready for marriage. He wasn't grown up enough. One thing I never realised was that he probably never will be. Years later he told me that it was best we didn't marry then 'because then you would have suffered like Marietta did, and I didn't want that for *you*.' I suffered later!

But at the time I was very upset. Then I got a letter from

Laughing All Over The World

Jean and Francis. Rick was still seeing Marietta 'and they're planning to get married in July'. I panicked and tried to ring Rick but each time I phoned, his Mum answered and said he wasn't at home. She'd get him to ring me back but he never did.

I knew when he was getting married so I took the week off work and sat by the phone willing it to ring. And I sat. And I sat. Finally, because I'd run out of everything from milk to soap, I made a dash down the road to the shop.

It goes without saying that in those ten minutes he rang. It was his wedding day and, on his way to the register office in Woking, he and his best man Peter Gibb, called round at my Mum and Dad's. He said to my Mum:

'Phone her while I'm here and if she answers …'

So Mum rang but I'd just nipped round to that bloody shop. Rick was wearing the blue velvet suit we'd already chosen for him to wear at our wedding before I left for Australia. But he must have put on a bit of weight because he'd burst the zip and the flies were held together with a safety pin.

'Take those trousers off,' my mum said. 'You're not going out like that.' He took them off and she mended the zip there and then, and off he went.

To marry Marietta.

5

Something About You Baby I Like

Marietta was very different from the girls the band were used to; she was rich, she was posh, she spoke five languages — but she was bang in love with Rick. She didn't do drugs, she drank rarely, except the occasional glass of champagne or finest German wine — and for a while Rick cleaned up his act. He was smitten, anxious to please — but still, after all, he *was* a rock star. It couldn't last long.

After their marriage, the couple moved into Lil and Dick's home which, for Marietta, must have been a culture shock and a test of her love. Then, with the band beginning to do well, they moved to a house in Woking.

I gather it was a happy time, especially when their first child, Richard junior came along. Rick was a dad, and he was thrilled. Ironically the rest of the band were all embroiled in marriage problems.

But, for Rick, old habits died hard. He'd been a good boy,

but he couldn't stay a good boy forever. He started boozing again and monogamy was never one of his strong points. The groupies were too tempting. There was one, a girl who worked in the cloakroom at The Marquee. Her name was Laura and Rick couldn't leave her alone. She was a nice accommadating girl, quiet, a bit on the chubby side, but friendly. And then there was always the adoring Janet who was never very far away.

For a long time after Rick's marriage I felt depressed. 'I've really blown it now,' I thought. Now there was no question of going back to the UK for at least another year. I couldn't face it.

I still got regular Rick Parfitt bulletins from my Mum and his cousin Sue. The band were going from strength to strength. I also heard from Jean Rossi. She didn't like Marietta, unfortunately no one did, poor girl, and all because they thought that she was, in some way, better than them. 'Marietta's got a really big nose,' Jean wrote, 'and she's very snobby.' That cheered me up no end. She said that Marietta didn't get on too well with the rest of Quo, mainly because she was from a completely different background. She wasn't 'our type' — whatever the hell type we were supposed to be!

I felt awful, but I still believed that even despite this marriage, Rick and I would end up together. The night I heard that Rick had got married I went out with my flatmate Kim and got totally wrecked. I woke up, still drunk, and we went out the next night and did the same thing. Then I started to date other men. But, even then, I couldn't bring myself to go to bed with anyone.

It was stupid, he was married after all, but I didn't want to get emotionally involved with anyone. It hurt, it hurt too much. It took about two and a half years before I'd make love to another man but even after that I was thinking of Rick.

But Jean told me the band were doing really well. Their trip to Australia had been a big success and it had worked well for Slade, too. I was pleased, especially for Noddy

Laughing All Over The World

Holder who's a lovely man. When I met him on that Australian tour we got on brilliantly, we'd sit in a corner and laugh our heads off — not because we were both stoned, but because we found each other funny. One night, en route to a gig on the Quo's Australian tour, a guy called Jimmy was eyeing me up. He actually asked Rick if 'he could bed me'. Rick, who'd been fuming because someone was chatting me up, said 'yes', to my horror. When Jim told me what Rick had said I was livid. I slapped Jim, then I slapped Rick and left for the gig with Chas Chandler, their manager, crying all the way on his shoulder. When Slade played, Noddy dedicated the song 'Darling, Be Home Soon' to me and I cried my eyes out again. That night Rick went off with someone else to 'teach me a lesson', and I went home alone. Cue for more sobbing. But I'll never forget how very kind Noddy was to me.

I kept writing to Jean and Francis, but suddenly their letters stopped. In the end, I tried ringing them at home but the number had changed. Then I heard that they had split up and when I next saw Francis in London a few years later, he sort of apologised about not writing.

'Jean couldn't lie to you in a letter,' he said, 'and say everything was rosy when it wasn't. It was bad. I was the one that messed up. I'd had enough, Patty. I'd been married since I was 17 and I'd had enough. I just wanted to be on my own.'

It was sad because by then they had three children. I'd always known that, despite the fact he sometimes played around, it was never remotely serious with anyone but Jean. He loved her desperately and vice versa, so God knows what went wrong. It was very sad for them all.

One thing the Quo have in common is that they'd never dump one woman until they had another serious contender lined up. Francis only left Jean when he met Liz, a lovely Irish girl, who worked for an Irish promoter. They met when the Quo were playing a gig in Dublin. They had a daughter, Bernadette. And he only dumped Liz once he'd lined up a beautiful Indian model called Paige. Then he moved on to

Patty Parfitt

Eileen who became the second Mrs Rossi. The girlfriends and wives need to overlap, because the men just can't cope on their own. They've never shared flats or lived alone. They simply wouldn't have a clue. They all need a woman to feed and clothe them – out of the nest they can't survive!

*   *   *

I spent two years in Australia and then I came back. Rick and Marietta had had their first child by then and that hurt — even more than when they got married. I didn't want to see Rick, but I rang his parents to say hello. They were almost like family to me.

Lil was out but Dick was pleased to hear from me.

'Lil's down the town with the boy, little Richie in his pushchair,' he said. 'If you go down the town you'll probably bump into them.'

'I might do that,' I said, having no intention of doing so.

'It's a funny marriage, Patty,' he said.

'What do you mean, funny?'

'It doesn't seem settled. I thought when the boy came along they would settle but they still haven't.'

I didn't ask any more, but I thought: 'Of course he's not settled! He's got to marry me!' And then I felt more certain than ever that one day we would get married.

I soon discovered that marriage hadn't changed Rick — he was still playing around. Even worse, on his wedding night he'd had to play a gig in Ireland and he'd ended up in bed with two girls — a sex sandwich! That's how Rick spent his honeymoon. Marietta spent hers with Dick and Lil!

In a way I felt sorry for Marietta. I knew that sharing a flat with Rick's parents wouldn't have been a bundle of laughs. Her parents were also furious when she married Rick, and they had cut her off without a penny.

I vowed that I wouldn't see Rick while he was married to her, however long that might be. I didn't want to get involved

Rick and I share a cuddle on board our boat, the Silversun, on the Thames.

Top left: Over indulging at a Quo gig in 1972 – the band had recently ditched their coiffed look, and were getting back to their hard rockin' roots.

Top right: Randwick Racecourse, Australia, 1973. Quo supported Slade – this was the first time I'd seen Rick since leaving the UK in 1972.

Bottom: A studio shot of Quo taken while I was in Australia.

Top: Quo get their first gold disc, 1974. From right to left Bob Young, Colin Johnson, Quo and assorted members of Phonogram management.

Bottom left: Just back from Australia for good, and so happy to be back with Rick. Cousin Sue stands on Rick's right.

Bottom right: The hard life of a rock star! 'Working' in Nassau.

Top: Out and about at the Hippodrome with Rick. No doubt it was another night of NIPS (Never Ending Inebriated Parfitt Syndrome)!

Bottom left: Posing outside the flat at Quay West on the way back from the rock festival at Knebworth. There is no one on the phone!

Bottom right: On holiday in Portugal – Rick was burned to a crisp!

Our wedding day, July 5 1988.

Top: Celebrating the wedding and Quo's Wembley gig at Stringfellows, with the man himself, Peter Stringfellow.

Bottom: Rick and I on the Silversun. That phone cost over £1000 by the time the HP had been paid off! And by then you could buy them for £30!

Rick Parfitt – the woman! Rick relaxes in Nassau, indulging in a favourite pursuit, dressing in drag.

Top: Quo rehearsing for Live Aid. These were Alan Lancaster's last rehearsals with them – although he was the last to know it.

Bottom: A sticky encounter with trifle while recording at Farm Place, Sussex in 1989.

in their marriage, and I certainly didn't want to be responsible for any problems.

But I hadn't been back long before Rick phoned me at my brother's. His Mum and Dad had told him I was staying there and first of all he just spent a couple of days driving up and down outside, just like he used to when we first met.

Then the band went away for a week or so to play some dates and when he came back he rang.

'Let's go for a drink,' he said. 'Just a drink.'

'OK,' I said. I could never really say no to him.

We couldn't meet for three days because the band were away. I was in a total panic. I kept thinking: 'Oh my God, I've put on weight and I've got nothing to wear. I look a right state!' So I starved myself for three days, I didn't eat a thing, and then I borrowed my dad's car and picked him up at the end of his road. He and Marietta had moved into a nice house in Woking by then, complete with its own private drive and swimming pool.

He slid right down in the front seat so no one would see him and we drove to Pyrford Lock on the Thames which was an old haunt of ours years earlier.

We had a drink and I asked him how things were going.

'Oh, you know,' he said evasively. 'It's just ticking over, it's all right. The kid's nice. He's lovely. I do my own thing and I expect she does hers, I don't know.'

He looked at me.

'I don't suppose you'd come on tour with me? Or away for a few days?'

It took a lot of self control but I said: 'No, you're right. I won't.'

'Oh come on, it's you and me. We're eventually going to be together, aren't we? What difference does it make?'

'No, I won't. If you do decide to finish with Marietta, you know, divorce her, then I'll be there but while you're still married this is the last time we go out.'

I knew how I'd feel if someone did that to me, and I didn't

Patty Parfitt

want to do it to anyone else. Now, ironically, I do know because that's just what Marietta did to me years later. She obviously didn't have the same scruples.

'I've got to go now — Dad wants the car back.'

'Yeah, I ought to go, too.'

Rick wanted to drive and promptly reversed into a tree, smashing my Dad's back lights. 'I'll pay for it,' he said. How was I going to explain this to my Dad? Of course I lied about it — vowing never to lie for Rick again.

He moved over and slumped down in the passenger seat and I dropped him off at the corner. He tried to kiss me but I turned my head so it ended up as a peck on the cheek. I knew what a kiss would lead to and I'd just get too upset.

I soon realised I couldn't stay in Woking. Rick was just too close. I could have walked to his house in six minutes. One day I saw the baby Richard in his pushchair. Lil had left him outside while she went into the corner shop. I knew immediately from his smile that this was Rick's son. Baby Richard looked at me and gave me that big Parfitt grin. I could have died, I felt quite sick.

I used to see Marietta striding along Woking High Street. In those days she always seemed to wear long, witchy black skirts, big black boots and hats — in Woking! She dyed her hair a lot — Rick obviously wasn't keen on her as a natural brunette — he does like his blondes.

Usually I ducked into shops to avoid her but once, when I was with Mum, she couldn't help but see me. She obviously knew who I was — she'd seen the photos Rick still had. She drove up in her Range Rover, stopped and stared at me. Then she tossed her huge nose in the air and drove off.

I really couldn't stand it much longer, so I quickly got a temping job in London but even that wasn't far enough away from Rick. Then I saw an advert in *Girl About Town* magazine for a nanny in New York. I applied, got the job and a month later I was off to the Big Apple.

It was a daunting experience. I had a cousin who lived in

Laughing All Over The World

upstate New York but, apart from her, I didn't know a soul. It was Australia all over again — in at the deep end. I was to be nanny to one of Dustin Hoffman's lawyers, Mr Freiburg. His wife had died of cancer a few years earlier and left him alone with two children, a boy and a girl, to look after. Before I arrived I hadn't even met him — the nanny who I was replacing interviewed me. She was leaving to get married to a New York cop.

The lawyer picked me up from the airport and we got on well. The kids were lovely — Richard and Lynn. Life seemed to be looking up for me although I still missed Rick desperately. But there I was in this huge New York apartment sleeping in what was called 'the library', with an original Picasso sketch on the wall. Mr Freiburg said it was worth half a million dollars but, even standing on my head I couldn't make much sense of it!

I got on well with the kids, and I had my keep plus about $100 a week spending money. I also had plenty of time off. There's a kind of mafia of English nannies in New York. My predecessor, now married to her cop, had opened a bar called Louis'. Her husband was only twenty-six but he'd been shot in the line of duty, so he was entitled to retire with a nice pay off.

I had a couple of drunken nights there when I got picked up, but nothing serious. I still couldn't bring myself to go out with anyone. It was ridiculous really but soon after arriving I had a telegram from Rick asking me to phone him when I got to New York. I hadn't even told him I was going but he must have been told by Cousin Sue who always acted as our go-between.

Rick's telegram said that Quo were about to do their first tour of the USA and they'd be playing New Jersey which, from New York, was just over the river. 'Please come and see me,' it said. But I had a problem; no transport. The boss was insuring me to drive his Mercedes so I could ferry the kids around, but the policy wasn't ready yet so I could hardly ask him.

Patty Parfitt

I looked up trains and planes but it came down to the fact that it would have taken me eight hours to get there and back, plus my whole week's wages. So, very reluctantly, I left a message at the gig to say I couldn't get there and would he please ring me.

Of course, I never heard a word and I was so depressed about it all that I went to Louis' bar, and then on to another bar with some friends. I got roaring drunk and ended up waking up in a flat in Queens with a man whose name I couldn't even remember. My eyes cracked open, my head pounding, and there was this attractive-looking blond guy putting on Lycra cycling shorts and top. It turned out he was a long distance cyclist who was off to race in a marathon! Since I couldn't remember a thing, including his name, I didn't like to ask if we'd had our own marathon the night before!

'Hi, honey,' he said. 'There's some juice and coffee over there on the bar. If you're going to be here I'll catch you later, if not leave your number and I'll call you tomorrow and we'll have dinner.'

I muttered 'Right' then off he went and I beat a hasty retreat. I never saw him again, and I never went back to that bar — I was grounded in Louis' bar for the rest of my trip. But I had a good time. At the weekends I'd go upstate and see my cousin, unless the boss wanted me to babysit. I grew very fond of the children and they loved me; the little boy used to bring me flowers, I think he missed his mum a lot. Lynn was the same and she wanted all the cuddles and love I could possibly give her.

They were the reason I extended my visa for another two months so I was there for eight months — another eight months without Rick.

But I still got the usual Rick Parfitt bulletins about what the band were up to and, from what Rick told me later, I was quite glad that I didn't meet up with them in the USA. It sounded like a nightmare. By now, at home in Britain and in

Europe, they were stars. It was a bit of a come-down to go to the USA and suddenly find yourself very small fish in a very big pond.

For some reason Quo never made it big in the States — I've never really understood why and I don't think they do either. Later the new management said it was old management's fault — and old management said it was because the band wouldn't take second billing any longer. Who knows? But America did get them heavily into something else — cocaine.

Of course, they'd tried it before but Rick told me that it was in America that he and Francis really took to cocaine in a big way. It coincided with his decision to give up smoking dope after he had a scary experience with a witch, supposedly a white witch, but she didn't sound very white to me.

While they were in America the band partied big time — Rick must have loved it. He met the witch, a hippy type, and she told him she had some really good dope back at her place. Of course, Rick didn't need asking twice, so back they went to her apartment where, obviously, they had other things to do. Then she turned him on to this really strong grass, which completely freaked him out. He was tripping and he didn't like it one little bit, he felt totally out of control, he was hallucinating. It wasn't fun any more.

It scared him to death and he said he made his getaway as fast as he could. Rick didn't like all the witchy things she said she was involved in, so he put it down to experience and moved on in his usual fashion.

But he hadn't heard the last of her. Just before the next gig she rang up and asked him for some tickets. Rick was so scared of her that he said no and she warned him that he'd regret it — she'd made a voodoo doll of him and was going to wreak revenge!

It sounds ridiculous but, once on stage, Rick was doubled up with pain and he was convinced it was where she was

Patty Parfitt

stabbing the voodoo doll. He felt ill for days afterwards and he's never forgotten it. For years he wouldn't smoke any dope at all — he just stuck with the cocaine.

But that piece of self-discipline didn't last long — and, of course, he never gave up the trolloping either! The white witch wasn't that powerful!

6

Ain't Complaining

In fact, as I found out later, the boys had a whale of a time in the USA. In fact, it changed their lives because it got off to a very good start.

They were met at Los Angeles airport by an enormous suited chauffeur driving an enormous black limousine. This was *style*, this was *the* way for Quo to arrive in America. And it got better.

They piled into the limo and headed out from the airport to the middle of town.

'Hey guys,' said the driver. 'If there's anything you guys need while you're here, you juz let me knowah ... and I mean *anything!*' and with that he flung open the centre cassette holder between the seats. It was full of drugs: coke, speed, hash, grass, everything you could think of.

The boys' eyes lit up.

'Cor!' said Rick. 'We'll have some of that!'

So the boys discovered cocaine and soon fell hopelessly in

Patty Parfitt

love with it, especially Rick. Even Francis preferred it to his constant flow of hash.

On their first night they were due to do a gig at the Whisky-A-Go-Go Club. They were backstage waiting to go on when suddenly the dressing door burst open and half a dozen scantily-clad young women burst in.

'Hi!' they said. 'We're the Little Angels. Are you guys the rock band?'

The boys from Peckham and Woking nodded enthusiastically.

'Can we suck your cocks?'

'Er, YES!' went the chorus.

'Does that include management?' said Colin Johnson, putting his hand up in the air as if he was at school.

'Sure, honey.'

There was a synchronised unzipping of flies and the girls expertly got to work. It didn't take them long.

'This is going to cost,' Colin Johnson was thinking. But no. Afterwards, the girls had a drink and a chat and handed out their business cards, on which were printed The Little Angels, together with their phone numbers.

'That was on the house, guys, any time you want a good time you just give us a call ...' And they were gone.

The boys looked at each other and laughed. Yes, they were going to enjoy America!

Professionally, however, it was disappointing. It was especially frustrating for Colin Johnson. 'Matchstick Men' had been a hit in America and people hadn't forgotten it. But they seemed reluctant to accept the band's new image and getting them airplay on the radio was proving a nightmare.

Even so, the American trip was memorable for Colin and changed his life, too. He was walking down a street in Los Angeles looking for a taxi rank, when a beautiful blonde came walking towards him.

'Excuse me,' he said. 'Can you tell me where I can get a cab?'

'Where're you going?'

'My hotel, the Hyatt on Sunset.'

'My car's here,' she said. 'Get in. I'll drop you.'

Her name was Helene. They had dinner, and the following day met on Santa Monica beach and decided to get married. Three months later they were both divorced, and eighteen months on, Helene moved to England and they were married.

The band didn't like her. Helene, they thought, was a looker but she was loud, a loud-mouthed American. And they thought she took up too much of Colin Johnson's time.

At one point Rick even said: 'It's her or us ...' but Johnson managed to smooth his ruffled feathers. Helene stayed — and the band stayed.

So the band returned to England sexually satisfied, stoned and tired.

Back home the band soon remembered that grass was nice but coke was better. But they needed someone who knew how to get it.

Fortunately they had hired a bloke called Ronnie Brown as a driver. He joined Quo for the princely sum of £40.00 a week plus £1.00 an hour overtime. Since the band hardly used the car during the day but always at night, Ron was happy.

The band set up a car hire company using Ron's organisational skills called Starfleet, with a Daimler, limousine and Bentley and in the summer Ron would drive Arabs around London. But apart from that his sole customers were Quo themselves and, in the end, he spent most of his time driving Rick — or getting him out of trouble.

Ron was a cheerful, discreet and generous. But he was much more than a driver. He knew a man who knew a dealer so he could get the boys their coke.

He was general factotum and on tour he even undressed Danielle, the mannequin, and took her legs and arms off, before packing her into one suitcase with her clothes in another.

Rick and Ron became good friends although Ron did get annoyed when Rick was late paying for his coke. But Rick was such a likeable bloke you couldn't bring yourself to be annoyed with him for long. Francis was snorting even more coke than Rick but always paid on the dot.

For a while, Rick and Marietta had seemed blissfully happy. But as Quo's fame grew so did Rick's intake of booze and coke until Francis and him were doing a couple of grammes a day — and, as he admitted later, he was treating Marietta appallingly. He called her 'The Doormat' and, Marietta told reporters later, occasionally beat her.

Of course, Rick couldn't bring himself to give up the groupies altogether — so another of Ron's assorted duties was ferrying Rick to and from groupies. One trip he made frequently was to a high rise flat in Kilburn where old friend, and long-time groupie, Laura from The Marquee lived with her Scottish mother. Rick was quite partial to her and saw her on and off for years.

As Quo became more famous, chatting girls up became obsolete. Instead they'd eye them up, decide which ones they wanted and then send Ron to inform them.

Most were dogs and one of the crew made a cut-out dog and awarded it to whoever of the band had been with the doggiest bird the night before. But the band had a logical explanation for going with dogs — you were less likely to catch anything because probably no-one else had been with her!

The *Rock Around The World* Tour was the biggest the Quo had ever done and they were beginning to believe that they really were stars.

Fame went to Rick's head, and he became very full of himself. The rivalry between Francis and Rick also intensified. Francis was always asking Rick to turn down the rhythm guitar amp, as it drowned out the lead guitar. Rick's response was to turn it up even louder. Francis went mad. On stage together, they'd be grinning away at each other, but were usually saying: 'Get out of my space, you bastard!'

Increasingly, unlike the old days, they didn't socialise together.

Once Ron picked Spud up from the airport and Spud asked Ron to drive him round to Francis'. Francis opened the door and said: 'What you fucking brought him here for? I don't want him in my house — take him away.' So, both feeling rather embarrassed, they went back to the car and drove off somewhere else.

As the money rolled in, Alan Lancaster began to put some aside, and seriously thought about moving to Australia and commuting to play with Quo. John Coghlan lived pretty modestly and Francis was shrewd. His beautiful house had only cost him £55,000 and was rapidly increasing in value. It also had a self-contained flat for his mum so she could live with him. She still cooked him breakfast every day! His beloved Koi carp, coke habit and a new BMW every year were his only extravagances.

But Rick was a different story. He loved spending his cash. Cars were still his first priority and the car showroom people could see him coming a mile off. He'd say: 'That sounds good, that's a great deal.'

And they'd grin happily and say: 'Yeah, Rick, it is.'

By this time, most of the band's marriages were going under. Of course, Francis had already split up with Jean and gone off with Liz, the promoter he met in Dublin. Alan had dumped Pat for Dayle and John Coglan had divorced his wife Carol and married Gillie.

But Marietta hung on in there. She and Rick now had two children — Richard junior and a beautiful little girl called Heidi.

Marietta really loved Rick. She knew that he was sleeping with other women, but she couldn't bring herself to make the break. Rick treated her appallingly, and it seemed they were destined for divorce eventually. But there was a final blow in store for them both.

7

Lonely Nights

I was in Sydney in the winter of 1980 when I bought a newspaper and practically dropped it in shock. I felt sick and horrified, and hurried home. The paper reported that Heidi, Rick's two-year-old daughter, had drowned in his swimming pool at home. I phoned England instantly. I couldn't get through to Rick but friends filled me in.

He was heavily into booze and drugs then. He told me later that he'd been watching *Match of the Day* in the sitting room with his son Richard. Marietta was in the kitchen, preparing lunch with Heidi when she said she wanted to go and see Daddy. So Marietta said: 'Off you go then, he's in the sitting room.'

But Heidi never got there. They had a little dog called Silky, which she adored — she used to follow it everywhere — and Rick reckons that she spotted the dog through the window and ran out after it. Maybe the dog jumped into the pool — he was wet — and she jumped in after it, or maybe she just fell in —

no one knows for sure.

Marietta went into the lounge and said: 'Have you got Heidi?'

'No,' Rick said, 'I thought she was with you.'

They stared at each other for a second, and then suddenly realised what had happened.

Rick flew out of his chair, pushed Marietta out of the way, and dashed down the garden to the pool. Richard had had the same accident just the year before and, terribly, it happened to our son, Harry, ten years later.

When Rick got to the swimming pool he saw Heidi floating on the surface, face down. He jumped in and got her out. Rick gave his little girl mouth-to-mouth resuscitation and Marietta called an ambulance. It came quickly, and they gave her oxygen, but she was dead on arrival at the hospital.

Of course, they blamed themselves, but really it was a terrible and tragic accident that could so easily happen to anyone.

Rick was absolutely devastated. He began to develop a phobia about water. For a long time after Heidi's death he wouldn't go in a pool at all. The first time was when Quo went to record a video in the desert in Bahrain. Part of the video showed the band in the pool. Rick told me afterwards that he was nervous — but he was fascinated by the water at the same time. Once he was in the pool he kept going under and holding his breath until Francis had to pull him up by the hair and told him not to be so silly. Later he'd do the same with me. I'd find him holding his breath under water in the bath and I'd yank him out. It scared the living daylights out of me.

He said that he wasn't trying to kill himself, he just wanted to hold his breath underwater to experience what it was like. He wanted to know what Heidi had felt.

I could understand it in a way. He wanted to experience what she might have felt. He was haunted by the fact that she suffered.

Laughing All Over The World

Heidi's life, death and funeral traumatised Rick more than probably anyone can guess. Marietta didn't want Heidi to have a funeral — she wanted it to be a wedding, a celebration of her short life. So her body was dressed up as a little bride. Everyone who came to the funeral had to wear white or cream. I thought it was sick but perhaps it helped them, perhaps it was one way for them to cope.

I rang Dick, Rick's Dad, to offer my condolences.

'Give my condolences to Lil and Rick,' I said. 'But don't tell Marietta I rang because she might think something's going on between Rick and me and there isn't, honestly.'

'I know,' he said, and he sounded heart-broken. 'I won't tell Marietta. Did you hear about the funeral?'

At the time I hadn't.

'It was awful,' he said. 'Awful. They dressed her up, Patty. She had a wedding. I've never known anything like it. Terrible.'

All the band attended the funeral and Francis was wonderful. As soon as he heard, he was round to Rick's — to be with him, all their differences forgotten. When it comes to the bottom line their long-lasting friendship is strong — even if they don't quite believe it!

Rick had been so out of it on booze and drugs that when he first rang Francis, Francis couldn't quite believe what he was hearing. Rick told him what had happened.

'Are you sure?' said Francis. 'Go away, and call back later. Do you know what you're saying?'

'Of course I fucking do,' said Rick, who was in a state of shock. 'I've just pulled her out of the swimming pool.'

And then he burst into tears. Poor Rick. He loved Heidi so much and he loved Marietta for giving him Heidi.

He said to me later: 'I felt more for her when Heidi was born, not Richard, although I love him too. When Heidi was born I felt more for her then than any other time in our marriage.'

Andrew Bown, Quo's keyboard player, wrote a beautiful

Patty Parfitt

song after Heidi died, called 'For My Little Girl'. Rick was very touched by that. I've often wondered why Rick didn't write a song for Heidi himself.

Perhaps to write about Heidi would just be too painful.

8

So Ends Another Life

For a while Heidi's death brought Rick and Marietta closer together. Heidi's room was kept just as it had always been when she was alive, the pretty wallpaper, the cushions on the bed embroidered with her name which Claire Brown, Ron's wife had made.

Rick made a real effort. Once, he even took Marietta to Covent Garden to the ballet — he knew she loved the ballet but it was hardly his cup of tea. She put on one of her beautiful taffeta dresses and he donned a tuxedo. Unfortunately Rick got the days wrong and they turned up to discover there was no ballet — so he took her to Stringfellows instead. He was trying.

But it was a bridge too far. His life had been shattered by Heidi's death and, in fact, he was trying to blot out the memory of that terrible day with massive quantities of booze, coke and women.

Ron frequently drove Rick off to Kilburn and his old

Marquee friend, Laura. Once, to Marietta's horror, he brought Laura back to Hydon Ridge when Marietta was entertaining her family on a visit from Germany. Rick was so out of it he didn't give a damn.

The groupies came and went. Then he met Dee Harrington whom he'd known from years before, still gorgeous. Even better, she was an ex of Rod Stewart's! And anything Rod Stewart could do Rick Parfitt could do better.

Rick became a frequent visitor to Dee's flat in Chiswick, London.

But the affair with Dee just about finished Rick's marriage. Marietta was in despair. One Sunday Marietta was packing Rick's clothes for a forthcoming tour. But Rick had gone AWOL. In a panic, she rang Ron.

'Where is he?' she asked. 'I have to know.'

'I think he's with Dee Harrington at her place in Chiswick,' said Ron. 'But I don't think there's anything going on.'

Usually, Rick asked the faithful Ron to cover for him, but he hadn't this time. He just didn't care any more.

Marietta was completely broken up. She was ironing Rick's stage clothes, tears streaming down her cheeks, while her mascara dripped on to the shirts.

Ron phoned Rick at Dee's.

'Look, you've got to get home, you've got problems.' He then went to Chiswick and practically dragged Rick out of the flat and into the car.

Ron always asked him: 'Why? Why do you behave like this?' But Rick would shrug, and mutter that he'd been a bit fed up. He'd had a good coke binge and he didn't love Marietta, so it didn't bother him.

By now, on tours, anything went. If Francis took Liz along he'd have two suites — so she didn't have to use his loo (one of his foibles) — and Rick would eye up the groupies as soon as he arrived. Ron was kept on his toes keeping the band in coke. Both Rick and Francis were heavily into it by then — once Francis even rang Ron on

Laughing All Over The World

Christmas Day to ask him to get some.

'Francis! It's Christmas Day!' said Ron.

'Exactly,' came the response.

If Francis didn't have Liz in tow then he wasn't averse to passing the time with a groupie himself. But the rivalry between Francis and Rick was getting completely out of proportion.

If Francis went off with a girl, then Rick would have to go off with her later *and* another in tow. It was a constant tussle for leadership of the band, with Francis and Rick trying to better each other all the time. It became ludicrous.

Even the ever-faithful Ron was getting exasperated. The worst time for him was on tour. He had gone to bed and Rick was safely ensconced up the hall in bed with a groupie.

In the middle of the night the phone rang.

'Ron, get here quick,' yelled Rick. 'You've got to get rid of her! Send her home.'

'But Rick, she lives hundreds of miles away! It's the middle of the night!'

Rick and the girl had begun to cuddle and kiss, when they suddenly discovered that the girl had started her period! Rick couldn't cope with that! He jumped off the bed and locked himself in the bathroom, while Ron came to his help and talked to the girl, made some excuses and found her another room in the hotel.

Sometimes the band didn't even bother going to their suites after the gig. They'd all sit in the coach fooling about and snorting all the coke they could lay their hands on.

The coke began to affect Francis' nose, wearing away the membrane between the nostrils. Pretty soon his party trick was to push a cotton bud into one nostril and pull it out of the other! It was gross!

They were spending an absolute fortune. At the time coke cost about £70 a gramme. When rehearsing, they often spent between £600–£700 a day.

It wasn't doing them any good, and sometimes they'd be on

Patty Parfitt

stage sweating like pigs. Occasionally, they couldn't even make it to the encore and then they'd get slow hand-clapped. Then they reverted to their original game-plan, waiting until the show was over.

Francis also started to drink. He never used to but now he was necking booze at top speed. When the band took a break before the encore he could down half a bottle of tequila before going back on stage.

The booze and coke made Francis open up a bit, instead of being almost silent. He was up and then he'd have to smoke a few joints to bring himself down again.

Once Rick got some 'coke' from a roadie but it turned out to be speed. Luckily Ron was with him, and looked after him. He was shaking and jolting — his heart was pumping like crazy and he was sweating buckets. It scared the shit out of him.

When the Quo were in London, Rick enjoyed socialising with other stars — especially the ones who enjoyed a line or two themselves — and there were plenty of them.

Jimmy White was a laugh. Rick and Jimmy used to play snooker — with a difference. They'd line the coke up on the side of the table. You took a line — you played a shot. They played some mind-blowing games! Rick claims that he always took Jimmy to the blue ball — often Jimmy wasn't on form!

Marietta knew she couldn't take much more — the groupies, the clap, and waking up to find he'd trashed the drawing room and thrown the three-piece suite in the swimming pool — she was close to breaking point.

Then finally, after two years of this kind of behaviour, she served him divorce papers and Rick moved out. They had been together about seven years. Even then she found him a cottage just down the road nice and close to his son Richard — and her, of course.

But if Rick cared, he kept it well hidden, and so the abysmal behaviour went on. Soon *Hot Gossip* dancer Debbie Ash was a regular visitor at the cottage and they embarked on a two-year fling.

For a time, Rick and Debbie got on famously. But then the relationship foundered, and Rick moved on.

There was always his old flame, Janet, and, of course, there was Laura. But Rick was looking for fresh blood and soon became involved with Page 3 model Debbee Ashby. She was a blonde, too, seventeen, and she looked good on his arm but, after a while, that relationship hit the rocks as well.

Rick sank deeper into depression, drugs and drink. Things weren't going well with the band. He and Francis weren't getting on at all — they even travelled to and from gigs in separate limos.

Rick was still at Hydon Ridge with Marietta when he discovered that Francis had built a studio at his home. Marietta wanted to record a few songs so Francis said she could use his studio. Rick was livid — he had his own studio at home. But, Francis' was a 24 track, Rick's only an eight track studio. So, seething with annoyance, Rick made his a 24 track, too.

Rick also had his suspicions about Francis and Marietta. And that did nothing for their working relationship. Later, Rick accused Francis, saying: 'You fucked my wife, didn't you? Well, did you shag Marietta?'

Always a man of few words, Francis looked at him and said: 'Well, so?'

And that really pissed Rick off.

Things were bad. As early as 1982 Francis had gone to Colin Johnson saying he'd had enough and wanted to pack the whole thing in.

That was the year that they booted John 'Spud' Coghlan out of the band. John was gutted after all the years they'd worked together. He later cheered himself up by selling his story to a tabloid newspaper.

Alan Lancaster was also getting on everyone's nerves, especially Francis'. His tendency to throw tantrums hadn't diminished either. At the Carlton Hotel in Bournemouth, the band were waiting in the foyer for the coach to take them on

Patty Parfitt

to the next gig. Alan ordered a prawn sandwich.

'Those aren't prawns — they're shrimps.'

'No, sir, they're prawns.'

'Fucking shrimps!'

'I think you'll find they're prawns, sir.'

So Alan threw the plate of sandwiches up the wall and along the corridor. Rick and Francis, despite being totally out of it most of the time themselves, thought this was juvenile behaviour.

A couple of years earlier, Alan also decided to sack Colin Johnson. Colin insisted that 'Rockin' All Over the World' should be the first single from the *12 Gold Bars* album. Alan disagreed and sacked him.

Colin rang Rick.

'I've been sacked,' he said.

'Eh?' said Rick, confused.

'Alan's just sacked me.'

'Oh, has he? What do you want to do?'

'Well, you can stay with him or come with me. But I'd like to keep things the way they are.'

'Oh right,' said Rick. 'Fine.'

And that was the end of that. But when Colin went to Rick in 1982 and said that Francis wanted to quit — by this time they were arguing so much they were hardly speaking — Rick hesitated.

'What do you want to do?' Colin asked.

'I don't know, man. I'll have to think about it. Maybe I'll go to Australia. Yes, that's what I'll do.'

'I think that would be a bad idea, Rick. You know what he's like. Francis might say he doesn't want to tour again now, but give it a few months and he'll be itching to get back on the road.'

Colin was worried but he let them stew for a while and then he came up with a brilliant idea. He persuaded Rick and Francis to do a tour of personal appearances — not playing their music, just sitting up there on stage, talking to their fans

Laughing All Over The World

about their lives and careers. They got about £2,000 a night, enjoyed themselves and by the end of the tour they were — almost — best mates again. Then Francis said: 'Why don't we make a record?'

'Yeah, why not?' said Rick, and Quo picked up again, just as Colin knew it would.

The Quo also got a brilliant money deal for new albums, so it was a dead cert that they'd stay together for at least a couple of years more.

Even after Colin's management cut, Rick and Francis stood to earn a fortune. They got a big advance as well and they'd get extra from publishing if they actually wrote the songs. But Francis benefited more than Rick because he wrote more than Rick.

Rick found writing difficult — but not because he couldn't do it. He was just lazy.

Jackie Lynton was an old rocker from way back. He had hit hard times and had become a painter and decorator so Rick asked him to come and paint his house. Rick heard Jackie singing a tune and asked: 'What's that you're singing, Jackie?'

'Just a song I've been writing.'

'Come in,' said Rick. Jackie came in and worked the song a bit — and it came out as a top-ten hit, 'Rockers Rollin'', with Rick's name on it as co-writer!

By 1984 Francis was moaning again, saying he wanted to quit — or at least quit touring — and this time he was serious. The band were still contracted to do several more albums but they embarked on the *End of the Road* tour and played what was supposedly their last gig at Crystal Palace Football Ground.

Rick was stony broke. Marietta had taken him to the cleaners. The remainder had gone on cars or up his nose. He was fed up. Debbee Ashby was no love match. He was stuck in a small flat in Battersea. Then he got banned from driving — again.

9

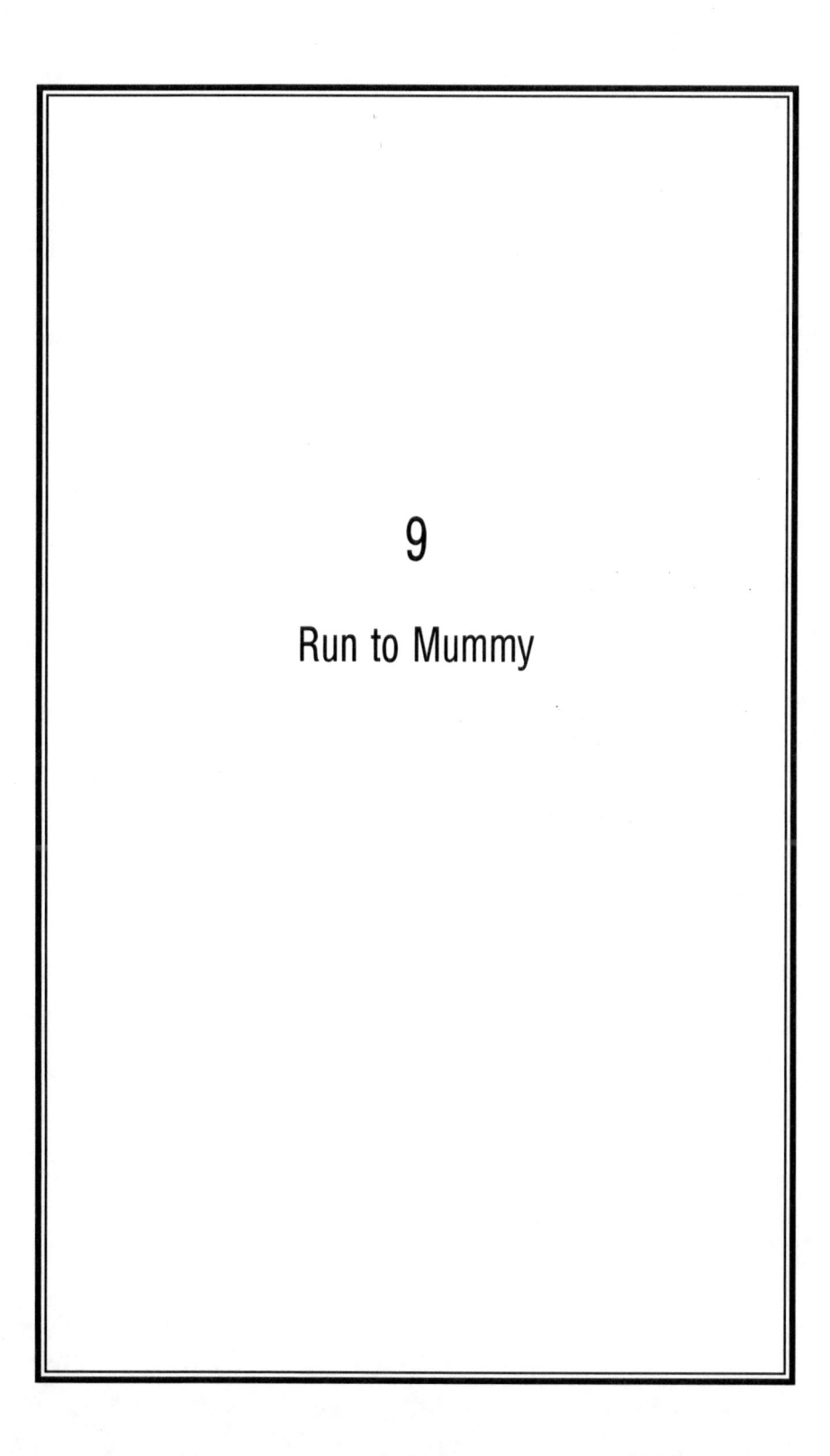

Run to Mummy

I knew Rick's marriage was in trouble. From what I heard, it had been wobbly even before Heidi died, right from the honeymoon, but after her tragic death, things just went from bad to worse. I felt desperately sorry for Rick and I longed to be able to comfort him. But I knew that he would be finding plenty of other women to do that, so I wasn't surprised when I heard that Janet was in the background again. There was always a strange link between those two.

Marietta went beserk when she found out that Janet had seen Rick after Heidi's death, and in one newspaper she later accused Rick of sleeping with Janet after Heidi died.

I honestly don't think that was true, although I know that Janet did go shopping with Rick to buy him a suit for Heidi's funeral. But that's all there was to it — just shopping and probably a shoulder to cry on. I never liked her, for obvious reasons, but I could understand that at times of tragedy you do tend to turn to old and trustworthy friends.

Patty Parfitt

It came as no surprise to me when I heard that Rick had been playing away from home with Dee Harrington, Rod Stewart's ex. Rick's always been jealous of Rod, even though when they've met up they're the best of friends. But Rick's always been envious of his success, and he's never been able to understand why he isn't the megastar that Rod is.

'I'm better looking than him,' Rick used to say indignantly.

Rick gave Dee some money for a flat, so he could visit her whenever he wanted and they settled for an apartment in Chiswick overlooking the river. Marietta didn't know anything about this but she'd ring up Claire, Ron Brown's wife, crying her eyes out and begging Ron to get him back.

I heard about this in Australia and, although I was jealous as hell because she was with Rick, I couldn't help feeling sorry for Marietta. It was a desperate situation. Half of me wanted to come home, but my instincts told me to hold off and wait just a little longer. As is often the case, instinct was right because then came the affair with Debbie Ash.

In the end, however, Debbie became dissatisfied with the situation and ended the relationship. It was the first time someone had dumped Rick and he was in shock.

Finally, I knew it was time to go home. I had a fashion shop now, which I could sell. Unfortunately, the week before I left, I stopped my insurance on the shop. A few days later someone smashed into the place and pinched all the stock. Replacing that for the new buyer wiped out most of my profit but I still had a few thousand left and booked my ticket for England.

I had to wait a month for my flight home, and I stayed at Melissa's house, a friend of mine. She'd gone to England for a few weeks' holiday and a strange coincidence occurred. Out of the blue Rick phoned me: 'Something very weird has just happened,' he said, hardly bothering to say hello after three years!

He and Colin Johnson had gone for a drink in a pub in Pimlico. By pure chance Melissa and her boyfriend had gone for a drink in the same pub and met Rick.

Laughing All Over The World

Melissa rang me afterwards too. 'I told him, "I can't believe it. I've just arrived in England, I've left your ex living in my flat and now I meet you!"'

Apparently Rick simply bought them a drink and said: 'Well, it looks like I'll have to marry her this time. The time is up.'

That same night I couldn't sleep. I couldn't get Rick out of my thoughts and I kept thinking: 'He's going to be there to meet me at the airport, I just know he is.'

In the morning, which was his night, the phone rang. I knew it was him. I'd even told my best friend Stephanie who was staying in the flat with me that he would ring.

'Go on, answer it,' she said. 'You say you know it's him, so prove yourself right.'

I did and of course, it was Rick. It was uncanny. I put on my phoney Australian accent and pretended to be someone else.

'Patty there?'

'Yeah, she's in the other room. I'll go and get her.'

That gave me a few minutes to collect my thoughts.

'Patty?'

'Yes.'

'Hello, girl,' he said, just as if we'd just met down Woking High Street!

I said: 'Ricky Parfitt! What on earth do *you* want? The weirdest thing is I knew you were going to ring.'

'But I bet you didn't know this. Colin and I went into a pub in Pimlico for a quick pint and bumped into your friend Melissa.'

Cue for gasps of disbelief all round, then Rick said:

'You're coming back?'

'Yes.'

'When?'

'July.'

'That's too long. It's June now. I can't wait that long, darling, you've got to come back now. Get a cancellation. I'll pick you up from the airport.'

Patty Parfitt

Well, I never could say no to that man. By lucky chance there was a cancellation on 23 June, 1985. I arrived back in England the following day.

The flight from Sydney arrived at Heathrow at 6.45am and all the way I was thinking that it would be a bloody miracle if Rick was awake at that time in the morning. But just to be on the safe side I made the most of the trip. As luck would have it, the only cancellation was a Qantas flight. I had a good friend, Amanda who I met while working as a driving instructor in Australia. She worked for Qantas, so I got upgraded to club class, and then it was champagne all the way!

One of the stewardesses I knew was also a beautician, so she did my face and hair and nails for me and just before we landed I changed into a very tight, long, black leather skirt and a suede top in a kind of rusty colour. That was a mistake as Rick told me almost as soon as we met: 'That should be shorter,' he said.

In fact, our first meeting at the airport wasn't a great success. I was trying desperately to make a grand entrance through Arrivals and, of course, I had a trolley for my luggage. I went through customs and out, but as I did the trolley wheel caught on a rubber plant pot, the wheel fell off, the trolley went careering away and crashed into a wall at which point I tripped and fell on my knees.

Angry tears fell down my cheeks which, of course, were bright red by this time and suddenly I saw these white trainers and black leather trousers, right in front of my nose.

'Well,' I said, 'that was a good entrance, wasn't it? I really can't believe I did that!'

'Hello, girl,' said Rick. 'Meet Ron,' and I looked up at big Ron, Rick's new driver. He muttered hello and as he looked down I could almost read his mind: 'Oh God, not another scatty blonde!'

Ron drove me and Rick to the Holiday Inn at Swiss Cottage where I was going to stay with Amanda for a couple of days until her return flight to Austrailia.

Laughing All Over The World

Rick spent most of the journey telling me how awful life was since he'd lost his licence for the third time and been banned for five years. I was looking at all the buses, amazed to be back in England, and scared to look at Rick for fear of the shakes! It's amazing that you can know someone for years and still get the shakes! It happens to us both — strange!

He explained that his divorce absolute had come through from Marietta and he'd gone out to celebrate, if that's the right word, with the girl known as Miss Whiplash on Kenny Everett's show. Foolishly, but as Rick was always wont to do, he'd taken the car. When he left the club he found a crowd of police waiting about for some reason. He tried to avoid them but they asked him for his autograph which Rick cheerfully gave — he's very good like that. They were all in a van and Rick had signed an autograph for every single one of them.

Then he walked off to the car which he'd parked around the corner.

Suddenly he saw the van was following him so he tried to do a bit of ducking and diving down different roads in London's West End. But it was no good. They cornered him in a cul-de-sac. He got out of the car and said to the coppers as they got out of the van: 'OK, it's a fair cop, guv!'

'You know you're well over the limit.'

'You bastards,' he said. 'I've given you all my autograph and you have the nerve to chase me.'

'No, mate,' they said. 'You're the fool.'

So they put him in the van and drove him back to the station while one of them followed in his car.

By this time Rick was sweating. What the Old Bill didn't realise was that Rick also had a gramme of coke on him. It was in a little white packet and he'd hastily thrown it on to the car floor as he was getting out of the car.

Somehow they missed it and after the formalities for drink driving he was allowed to ring Colin. It was the middle of the night and Colin wasn't pleased but he was quite used to it.

Patty Parfitt

This time Rick asked him to come and pick him up.

'Rick,' said Colin patiently. 'It's 4.00am. Crash out there for a few hours and then I'll come and get you in the morning.'

'Oh,' said Rick sulkily and then, pissed as a rat, slept peacefully in a cell for a few hours until Colin arrived.

Rick was furious about the driving ban. He always took his bans as a personal insult even though he knew full well he'd been in the wrong. And if there's one thing Rick hates, it's being without a car.

Once at the Holiday Inn, Ron grabbed some breakfast. I sat down, exhausted, in the lobby and Rick put his feet up on the sofa, his head on my lap, moaned that he was tired and promptly went to sleep.

Finally he left, I slept and the next day Amanda and I went to see my Mum and Dad who'd moved to Swindon. Fortunately, Dad lent me his car which I brought back to London. When he saw it, Rick's eyes lit up. A car! Pity it was an Allegro — but it would have to do.

'Come to the studio with me,' he said, 'and stay the night.'

Rick was recording his first solo album. The band had supposedly split, or at least they weren't going to tour any more, although they were still contracted to do some albums. Francis had done his solo album which flopped (to Rick's satisfaction) and now Rick was doing his and, typically, it was determined that it was going to be better.

I got to the studio, met the producer, Pip Williams, and Rick said: 'Sit down, I want you to listen to this track.'

I listened and it hit me — it was all about me coming back from Australia and although I know I'm biased, it was good, too. He dedicated the track to me and I was thrilled. It was called 'Show Me the Way'! In fact, the whole album was good, at least I thought so.

It was called *Recorded Delivery*. It had some great rock and some beautiful ballads. Some songs have been used as B sides for Quo, songs that really deserved to be A sides, but the record company, for whatever reason, only release singles with Francis singing lead. They say that Rick's voice is not as recognisable as Francis', which is weird because Rick sings at least half the songs when the band are on stage.

But Rick's album is great, I'd buy it despite our current situation. There are still a lot of songs that haven't been used and I really believe that he should write some more and get it released. It would be a great shame not to.

But, at that time, Phonogram had had troubles with Francis' solo album. Francis seemed to have lost his rock 'n' roll. It had just drained away over the years. Rick and I called it roundabout music. Another solo album of his flopped last year, too. But after the first failure Phonogram weren't keen on Rick's album. He was absolutely gutted when they axed it.

It was his first chance to get away from Francis, and be a star in his own right. While he was working on that solo album he was a changed man — he was more alert, and much happier. He felt he wasn't in Francis' shadow any more and that meant a lot to him. The rivalry between them at this point was worse than ever before.

Francis is so different from Rick — it's amazing that they've been together all this time. Francis doesn't like to go out — Rick *needs* to go out. Francis stays at home and he's quite happy, but he is very possessive about Quo. He hated it that Rick took some of the limelight off stage, and that Rick was so often in the papers. But on stage Francis always made sure he was the main man. Rick was rarely allowed to speak to the audience — Francis made that clear. Rick always wanted Francis to be a bit more flamboyant on stage. If they were abroad, he always wanted Francis to say: 'Hello, how are you? Good to be here,' in the local language. The audiences appreciated it if you spoke to them in their own language even if was just a few words.

But Francis wouldn't have any of it. He was never big on audience interaction. It was a missed opportunity really and constant source of irritation to Rick.

Patty Parfitt

So going solo would have been great for Rick.

But at the studio that day, we were happy as Larry. Rick told me he had a flat in Battersea overlooking the river — which sounded very glamorous — but I knew it only had two bedrooms and Alan Lancaster was staying with him.

Alan was over from Australia for Live Aid and the band were busy rehearsing for the concert, which was in ten days' time. It was good to see Alan again but Rick had obviously had a quiet word with him and during the evening Alan announced that he was going off to stay the night with his brother, so Rick and I were alone. I was as scared as hell and got the shakes again. Rick was nervous, too, I could tell. It was ridiculous. We were like two teenagers on a first date.

I was fully prepared for a night of passion but I should have known better.

We sat on the sofa and kissed. It was so good to be back in his arms and Rick nuzzled my ear. 'I'm not going to make love to you tonight, I want to, but not until the time is right for both of us.'

Oh shit, I thought. The same old story and I wondered whether he had the clap again. So we had a cup of tea and went to bed. I put on one of his old t-shirts and he took a large sleeping tablet, we cuddled up and both slept like logs. I was actually relieved — and I wasn't surprised.

Since meeting Rick all those years ago I have always loved kissing and cuddling. In fact, I could live on that alone quite easily without the rest! Rick used to tell me that I had a body you could get an electric charge from and he was quite satisfied with that. He said he needed that electric charge.

It seemed strange but after a while I began to accept our rare love-making days and settled pretty much for my cuddles. I was deeply in love with my man. Sex was not a priority for me or Rick, we felt we had something beyond that.

It used to scare Rick sometimes when I used to finish his sentences or answer him *before* he had spoken. I could read him like a book — still can! He used to buy something and say: 'You needed that,' before I'd even thought about it. He was always right. It was spooky at times and we used to say to each other: 'Get out of my head — I want to say that!'

But I have to say that those early days when I first got back from Australia were magic. We were together again just as I'd known we would be and Rick was wonderful. He bought me roses every week – he'd never bought me a daisy before – we held hands everywhere, we visited my Mum and Dad and visited his parents, too. It was like the old days and I loved it.

And when I saw the rest of the band it was like old times, too. I'd spoken to Francis on the phone when I was in Australia. I had rung the Quo office to tell them my flight details and Francis came on the phone.

'Looking forward to seeing you,' he said. 'I still think you're mad coming back to him but I'm looking forward to seeing you anyway.'

I could hear Rick yelling in the background: 'You're not bloody seeing her, I am, so you can pack that in!'

Rick came on the phone and said: 'Bloody Francis!'

'He just said he was looking forward to seeing me.'

'I know what he meant — and you're not going to see him anyway.' I'd told Rick years before about those kisses Francis and I had shared, and he was displeased to say the least.

So I said: 'Yes, Rick.' When he was in that kind of mood it was always best to agree.

In fact, I did see the rest of the band at a Nordoff Robbins awards dinner we went to four days later — all except Spud that is, who'd been sacked. It was a shame because I always liked him and we got on fine. But they said he became totally unreliable. He wouldn't turn up for gigs or recording or, if he did, he'd be very late. After the sound check Francis would always sneak back on stage to check that Spud's drums had been tuned correctly, because he didn't trust him to do it properly.

In Spud's place was a guy called Pete Kersher, who was lovely, and Andrew Bown, a very professional session

Patty Parfitt

musician who was the keyboard player. I'd met him before when Quo toured Australia for the second time.

I'd been in Rick's flat for a week. My suitcase was still on the bedroom floor and I was literally living out of it, but Rick said: 'Stay with me for a few days and we'll see what happens.'

'Fine,' I said. 'That'll give me a chance to look around for a flat of my own.' He gave me one of those Parfitt looks. He didn't like that.

To be honest, his own flat was a bit of a disappointment. The position was wonderful, right on the river with lovely views, although at that time the Chelsea Harbour was being built immediately opposite and it was a tip for a while.

At Valiant House, where the flat was, the actor Jack Hedley lived next door and Baroness Chalker had a flat on the floor below. But it wasn't that posh. There were two bedrooms, a bathroom, dining room and lounge. Rick had rented it furnished and the furniture was amazingly tacky — I soon changed that with Claire Brown's help!

I wasn't quite sure what the situation was — whether to go or stay. I had some money left over from selling my fashion shop in Sydney so I started looking around at flats nearby for myself, without telling Rick.

It was a fruitless search. Some of the places I saw were dreadful — either beautifully furnished but terribly small or large and really dark, unwelcoming and over-priced. I was beginning to panic. I couldn't really afford London — I would have to go back to the country or find a grotty bedsit.

One day I came back from flat-hunting and I was rummaging in my suitcase for something to wear that evening.

Rick marched into the bedroom.

'That's it!' he said. 'While you've been out I've emptied those drawers and I've made some space in the wardrobe. You're staying Patty. OK?'

'OK.'

He put his arms around me. I've always loved it when he

does that. I melted instantly.

'I want you here. Besides,' he added. 'I need you with me for Live Aid. So let's go shopping!'

10

Rockin' All Over the World

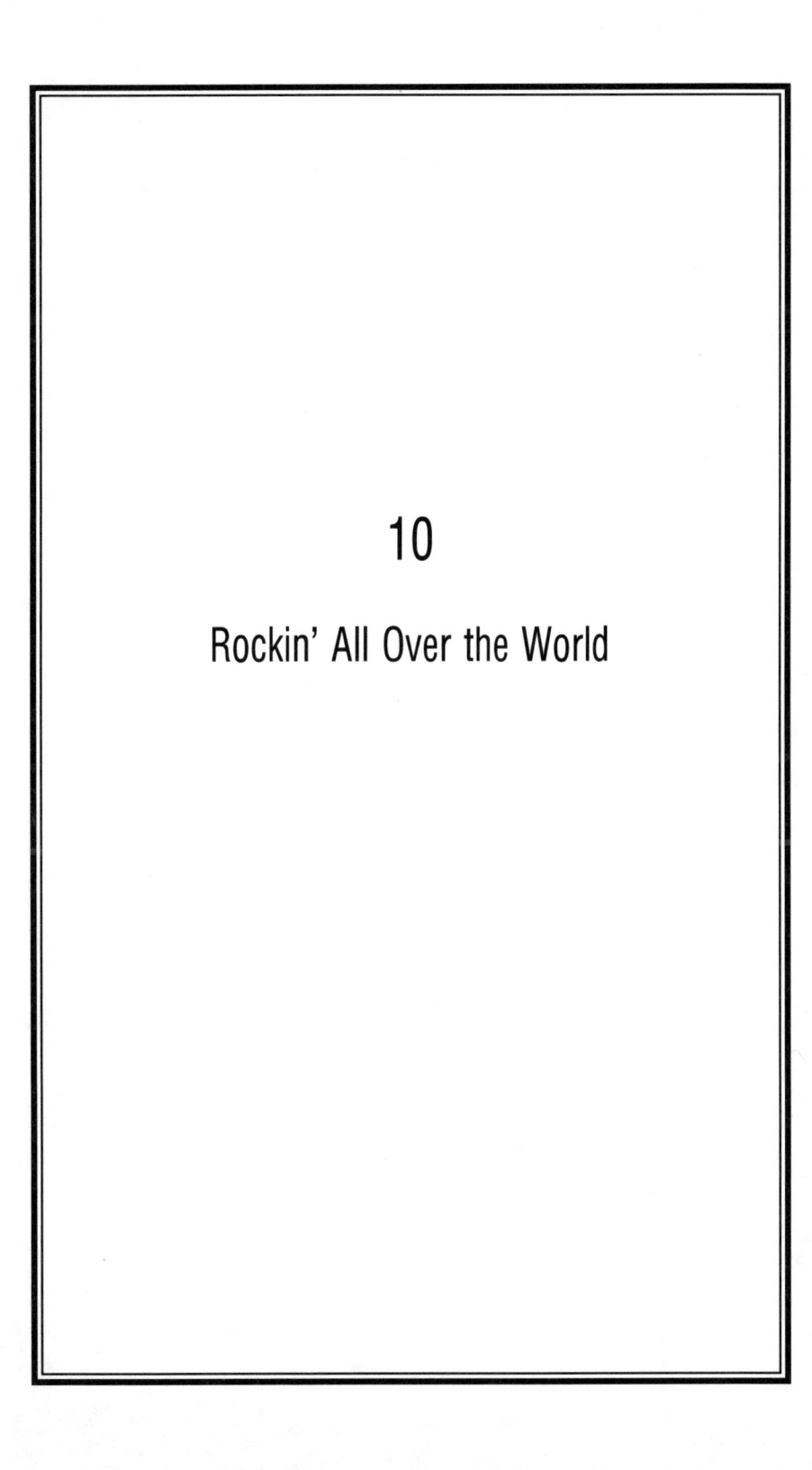

July 13 1985. This was Live Aid. Bob Geldof's brainchild after he was moved to tears by pictures of starving African children on the news. It was the biggest gig the world had ever seen with an amazing line-up. Millions of people would tune in on TV. The aim: to raise millions to help people who were starving to death in famine-wracked Ethiopia.

Quo had officially finished playing live but they were back together for Live Aid. What better number was there to kick off this phenomenal world event than 'Rockin' All Over the World'? For me, just back from Australia — and back with Ricky — it was magical. Nothing has topped it since – apart from Harry.

The band had been rehearsing hard for Live Aid and had done several promos for it. They were really excited — no one had ever been involved in a concert like it.

I was thrilled to bits because Rick was taking me with him. Rick was dead excited, too, although, like the rest of the band, he tried to act supercool.

Patty Parfitt

We were in Battersea, and just down the road from the heliport, so the band all turned up at our flat first thing and had a cup of tea. Noel Edmonds part owns the heliport at Battersea and he'd arranged helicopters for many of the bands to get to Wembley.

Ron was organising the cars for Quo at the gig itself and most of the crew were already there setting things up. So Francis went in one helicopter with Nuff and a couple of the Moody Blues and I went with Rick, Colin and Justin Hayward and John Lodge of the Moody Blues in another. I'd never been in a helicopter before but I didn't have time to get nervous.

All the stars were being ferried in to the Wembley Conference Centre to meet Prince Charles and Princes Diana. Then coaches or cars would take them to the stadium.

Rick had insisted I had something new to wear and took me along to Brown's in South Molton Street. I was a bit embarrassed because I knew money was tight. He was on a £100 budget at the time. The electricity, gas and phone were forever being cut off, and I always seemed to be running down to the bank or post office and trying to get us re-connected, my savings from Australia draining away all the time.

But Rick insisted on a new dress. He'd already asked Alan Lancaster if he could borrow some cash.

I said to Alan: 'You know he can't afford to buy me a dress. I've got some money — I can use that.'

Alan just shrugged. 'Don't argue — accept it.'

I said the same to Rick but he would have none of it.

'No, this is a big do and I want to get you a dress. You won't be able to afford the kind of dress I'd like you to have. Alan has lent me the money and I'm selling him a couple of guitars. Don't argue!'

So we trotted off to indulge in one of Rick's favourite pastimes — shopping. The dress cost £400. It was short, of course — very. A little blue/mauve fitted dress with sequinned straps. It was very pretty and not as tarty as Rick's usual taste. We chose pearl high heels to go with it and they were lovely.

Laughing All Over The World

The dress was for the evening. In the morning when we left for Wembley, I was dressed in jeans and t-shirt like everyone else.

The helicopter journey was great. From the air we could see the crowds of people already gathering and there seemed to be hundreds of helicopters behind us. I had a camera with me so I asked the pilot if he could fly low over the crowd so I could take some photos.

'Can we just go round once, can we just do a lap?'

'Yeah,' he said. 'No problem.' I got some great pictures. Rick seemed embarrassed as if this was very uncool but I didn't care. Afterwards, I was the only one who'd thought to take photos, and everyone was asking for copies!

The organisation was fantastic — no wonder Bob Geldof looked so exhausted that night. All the bands were gathered together in one enormous room which had been cut up into little alcoves — all the bands had their own little space. It was an amazing collection of people and, bearing in mind how temperamental rock stars can be, I was amazed that they'd all got there — on time — and none seemed to be playing up. The atmosphere was really friendly and happy. Being organised by a rock star who had been known to throw the odd tantrum himself saved a lot of problems.

Colin and I went off to the canteen to get some bacon sandwiches and coffees and, as we were going, someone came up to us and showed me a newspaper. And there was a picture of me and Rick in the beer garden at the Raven, down the road from the flat.

The headline was PARFITT PAIR BACK TOGETHER AFTER FIFTEEN YEARS. A photographer had taken pictures of us a few days before, John Blake did the interview; they must have held it back for Live Aid. I was pretty chuffed, and Rick was too, although, as usual, he pretended he wasn't.

As soon as we'd finished the bacon sandwiches we were all ushered upstairs to meet the Prince and Princess of Wales. Rick stood by the door and said: 'I'm going to be the first to

Patty Parfitt

meet her!' Everyone really wanted to meet Diana instead of Charles. He met her many times after that and she always said to Rick, laughing: 'Oh, you again!'

So we formed this kind of massive queue — apart from the bands, there were all the managers, wives and girlfriends. Francis stood next to Rick. Rick told me to get in line.

'I can't! I can't — I'm wearing jeans!'

But Rick grabbed me and pulled me into the queue. Helene, Colin Johnson's wife, was standing next to me, and Rick told her to keep me there.

'Patty,' Helene bellowed in her Texan drawl, 'just stand still and don't be so silly!'

So I stood in the line-up next to her and said to this chap next to me: 'Oh God, my legs are going to go.'

I didn't see who it was, but he said, 'Don't worry, I'll look after you.'

I looked again and it was Adam Ant. He was sweet, ever so kind to me.

I couldn't believe that I was about to meet the Prince and Princess of Wales, when I'd only just come back from Australia.

'Oh, I can't believe it, I shouldn't be here!' I said.

'Why not?' laughed Adam. 'You were in the papers today, I saw you. You're a star for the day and I've approved it! Look, if you feel your legs going I'll hold you up!' and he put his fingers in my belt loops. Suddenly we heard a drumming sound and the doors opened. The Prince and Princess of Wales were coming in.

Prince Charles went along the line first and I saw him talking to Rick and Francis, then Nuff, Andrew, Pete and Colin. The other stars, like Elton and Freddie Mercury who were opposite looked on. He shook hands with everyone. Seeing him in the flesh was a bit of a shock because he smaller than I'd imagined.

I curtsied. So did Helene. But hers was a typical, huge American kind of curtsey. If I'd done a big one like that I

Laughing All Over The World

would have been on the floor and he would have seen Adam Ant holding me up by my loops.

'Are you girls singing here tonight?' said Prince Charles looking at me and Helene.

I laughed and Helene said: 'No, my husband is Colin Johnson who manages Status Quo, did you see them down there?' and she looked down the line and went 'Cooo-eee!' How embarrassing!

'We're not appearing,' I said to the Prince. I looked down the line. 'They're my boyfriend!' He looked puzzled. Oh God.

'No, not all of them!' Oh God, he thought I was a groupie! The more I tried to talk my way out of it the worse it got. 'No, I mean the blonde one, Rick — he's my boyfriend.'

Prince Charles smiled. 'I hope you have a lovely time.' And he moved on.

Oh God, Rick, I thought, I told you I shouldn't be here.

Then Diana came along the line and everyone seemed to relax. She was lovely and very nice. Helene did her grand curtsey and I just shook hands and bobbed.

Diana had a wonderful smile.

'Isn't it exciting?' she said.

'Yes, it is, isn't it.'

She had an instant warmth. It was quite extraordinary. You instantly felt that you could relate to her, pop around for tea and a chat!

'I shouldn't really be here,' I spluttered. 'I'm not playing — I'm just Rick's girlfriend.'

She grinned at my cheekiness. 'Great! I can't wait for it to start,' she said.

Then somebody said: 'I'm sorry, but we must move on, Your Royal Highness.'

She looked around: 'Just a minute,' she said and when she turned back to me she smiled again: 'They're always pushing me around! It was very nice to meet you,' and she moved on.

Little did we know the hell she was going through then. She certainly didn't show it. She looked stunning and not too

137

Patty Parfitt

skinny, at least I didn't think so. I'm sure Rick approved! She went further down the line and was talking to someone else. I saw a man who was following her gently push her on. She frowned at him.

Then she turned back and looked at me, smiled and raised her eyes to the ceiling as if to say: 'See what I mean? They're always pushing me around!'

Afterwards Rick was agog: 'What did she say to you? She spent a lot of time talking to you.'

'Nothing much. We were just talking. She's really nice.'

All the bands were ushered off, and then coaches took us off to the stadium. Rick was sitting with Francis — probably to keep up appearances — although the great atmosphere was catching, so perhaps he actually wanted to be in Francis' company for a change! I went further down the coach and sat next to my new friend Adam Ant. Rick didn't like that at all, and before the coach had set off he'd collared me.

'I saw you talking to him in the line-up.'

'Well, he was standing next to me. I wasn't going to ignore him, was I? Besides he was holding me up because my legs were going.'

'Oh yeah, how was he holding you?'

'By my belt loops.'

'Not by the crotch of your pants?'

I looked at Rick. 'No, Rick.' He looked away.

On the bus, he kept looking around and giving me cross, jealous looks. Rick can be very insecure at times.

We all disembarked and Rick and Francis were immediately pounced on by reporters who wanted a few comments from them. I walked on, chatting with Adam, and we had to go down some stairs. I had high heeled boots on so Adam held my arm going down the stairs, just to make sure I didn't fall. Suddenly Rick, who had overtaken us, turned around and went beserk.

'*My* arm, I think,' he said to Adam and whisked me off.

I bumped into Adam later.

Laughing All Over The World

'You OK?' he said.

'Don't worry,' I said. 'Rick is funny at times.'

'I think he wanted to have a word with you,' Adam replied. But after that I kept my distance. It was obviously upsetting Rick and I didn't want that, especially not on that day.

Bob Geldof had insisted that, irrespective of the time each band went on, they all had to be at Wembley for 10.00am.

There were no excuses accepted. You were there on time or you didn't go on.

Everyone was playing for free but if you went one minute over your allotted time you had to pay £500 because that's what it was costing in air time. It was a great incentive! Rick, a great time-keeper himself, could relate to it!

Phil Collins was due to play Wembley and then fly to America to play there which was a great idea. In fact, Quo were asked to do it, too, but Rick and Francis didn't really want to. Rick thought it was all happening in London, not Philadelphia so Quo should stay in the UK. Francis didn't want to go because Quo weren't big in America, and he was worried that they'd be overshadowed by the Tina Turners of this world.

Even so, I thought it was a shame. Not because I would have gone as well, but because it would have earned them a lot of credibility in the USA.

The area behind Wembley stadium had been turned into an amazing caravan park, full of beautiful plants and grass.

Geldof had insisted that no one could leave until they'd played their piece, so the bands had to hang around. But that was hardly a hardship. Every band had their own luxury caravan and their own booze tent. The caterers came round continually making sure that there was enough food and booze and, of course, there was a lot of marijuana and coke from the dealers. It was all very civilised! But most of the bands stayed on the straight and narrow until they'd played their set.

I'm not so sure about Phil Collins. It was well known that he was extremely partial to coke. The joke doing the rounds of

Patty Parfitt

the caravan village was that he didn't need Concorde to get him to America to play the second half — he could have flown there on his own!

It was all a bit of a rush when we got to the caravan site because Quo were first on, so I rushed up with the other girls to our seats behind the Royal box to watch them.

It was quite an amazing moment, the atmosphere was so heady, everyone happy and pulling together. Bob Geldof and Paula Yates were sitting in the Royal Box with Charles and Diana and we sat a little behind them.

Everyone sang the National Anthem and the guards played at noon. Then in a few minutes Quo were on singing 'Rockin' All Over the World' and the crowd went mad. The roar from the crowd was deafening. Diana was on her feet dancing, and Charles was on his feet having a go, too — it was truly fantastic. I had goosebumps.

Quo were at their best and they played a great set. When they'd finished I wanted to stay and watch but I had to get back to meet Rick at the caravan. Those were my orders. Rick didn't want me out there on my own and, now that he'd finished, he'd be just hanging about so he needed me on his arm. I didn't mind; I was so proud of him, I smothered him in kisses and praise. And Rick was loving it, he was in heaven.

Now Quo could have a drink so they got stuck in and we had a lot of fun in this bizarre caravan village. Rick had the idea of getting everyone's autograph so we could keep a book as a souvenir. It was a good excuse to go around and say hello to everyone.

Everyone was there for Bob's dream, and we all had the utmost respect for him for organising Live Aid. There were no tantrums and no clashing egos; everyone did their bit and the atmosphere was terrific.

We managed to watch The Who play from side-stage and that was a highlight of the day for everyone. It had been years since they'd played live — clever Bob. Socialising in the village was great fun, too. We bumped into Paula and Bob,

Laughing All Over The World

and their eldest daughter Fifi who was then about four or five.

To be honest, he looked terrible, haggard and pale. I'm sure he wasn't stoned — he couldn't have coped with it all if he had been — but the poor man probably hadn't slept for weeks. He was probably just high on adrenalin. He had his first drink when he was on stage because, before that, he just couldn't risk anything going wrong; everything was timed to the second. Wherever he was Paula was with him, clinging on to his arm with love — at least that's what it looked like then.

In the afternoon Rick and I got the helicopter back to Battersea to get changed and prepare for the evening.

David Bowie was coming back with us because he wanted to go to town, too, and he brought along his girlfriend of the time. A curtain separated our seats from his and, as soon as we took off, strange noises came from behind the curtain. There was a lot of giggling and grunting! Rick just grinned and put his arm around me and the pilot kept right on flying!

From the heliport we went straight to the Raven pub where Rick was greeted like a hero. Everyone had seen Live Aid on telly and we collected about £70 which we topped up to £100 and took back to give in later.

Rick and I had a shower, and I changed into the little mauve dress. Rick put on his ebony blue silk suit, and then we got the helicopter back for the evening session. Back in the caravan village the party was in full swing, the ones who hadn't been on stage were gasping for a drink and the ones who had were getting stuck into the champagne.

We wandered around the village just soaking it all in and Rick said: 'Oh, there's McCartney!'

I'm not easily impressed as I've met so many rock stars over the years, but Paul McCartney has always been my hero.

Rick and Paul greeted each other like long-lost friends with Paul teasing Rick: 'I know who you are!' Rick introduced me and Paul said: 'Oh, I know who you are, too. I saw you in the paper this morning!' He was absolutely lovely.

Paul was with Linda. She came over and was very nice and

Patty Parfitt

friendly, but Paul kept staring down the front of my dress. I didn't have big boobs at that time but he kept speaking to them!

Paul winked at me and Rick promptly put his arm around me. But he wasn't jealous of Paul. As he explained later: 'He's a Beatle — he doesn't count!' Then it was time for Rick and Francis to have their photo taken by David Bailey, the top photographer.

Rick didn't want to leave me alone, so he asked George Michael to look after me while he had his picture done.

George could hardly say no. Anyway he was trapped, he was due to have his photo taken next, so he said: 'Sure.'

'I'm really sorry about that,' I said. 'I'm a big girl now, I can quite easily look after myself.'

But he just laughed and we got chatting. He was a nice guy.

'Are your parents here?' he said. 'Mine are, but I've lost them.'

'No, but I think my brother and sister-in-law are somewhere about.'

We chatted about family things until Rick came back, and then George went off to have his photo done.

'All right, girl?' said Rick.

'Fine,' I smiled.

'I left you with George because I knew you'd be safe with him — he's gay.'

'He's not!'

'He is.'

I wasn't sure whether to believe Rick or not — he tends to think every man he meets is gay — especially if they're good-looking. But, as time would tell, he was right!

Suddenly it was time for the finale. Quo's joke was that they were going to sing 'Feed the Worms' which was a bit sick. But rock stars, especially Quo, aren't renowned for the subtlety of their jokes.

They all trooped up to go on stage and I stood at the side,

off stage. Rick grabbed me. 'You're coming on,' he said.

'I'm not!' I said. 'It was bad enough going in the line-up but I can't go on there!'

'Look,' he said, 'It's only this crowd of people. Come on.'

'Oh yeah,' I thought. 'Only this little crowd of 80,000!'

He pulled me on, but our hands separated in the crush and I ended up standing in front of Elton's piano, right in the middle — at the front! Rick was behind with his arms wrapped around me. Bob Geldof was up in front doing his thing to the crowd: 'Come on, come on, I can't hear you! Feed the what?! Shout a bit louder!'

Different stars were taking the microphone to do their own bit of the song. I still had a glass of vodka and tonic in my hand, because I wasn't expecting to be on stage so I made my way to the piano to put it down. Just as I did so, Paul McCartney passed the microphone to George Michael, beside me, and suddenly he's wearing my vodka and tonic all the way down the front of his trousers. Ooops!

There was George doing his bit, with me dying of embarrassment and shuffling to get out of the way as much as I could. But it was a real crush, so in the end I just had to stand there, join in and smile like everyone else. In fact, you couldn't stop yourself smiling. It was such a good atmosphere. We had face-ache, as Rick and I say, all night!

It was such an incredible sight — something like 80,000 people out there, many of them lighting candles and the emotion of it all was getting to everyone.

I stumbled — everyone was jostling everyone else — and David Bowie held me steady as we looked out at that incredible sea of people.

'A lot of people out there, aren't there?'

'It's amazing,' I said, quite frozen to the spot.

'Just think, there are about 80,000 people out there and there's 20 million more watching us on TV.'

'Fantastic, isn't it?' he said.

'Yes,' I said, 'er ... fantastic.'

Patty Parfitt

And he was right — it was. As the song ended, I turned around, and David let go of me and gave me a big grin. It's hard to describe how everyone felt that night. Everyone was on a high — not because of the booze, or the drugs, although there was plenty of that about (and Rick swore that just about everyone was on coke), but just at what was happening, all those people coming together and in the right spirit. That might sound corny today. But it was great to be corny.

Everyone took a bow and, six encores later, left the stage and then there was a bit of a party backstage. But that didn't last long. Everyone had a drink or two, but Bob had organised that as well. I still find it amazing that I'm actually in *The Official Live Aid* book.

There were cars or coaches to take people where they wanted to go. Most of us didn't want to stop partying. It had all gone so well, everyone was still high on adrenalin and the nightclub, Legends, had been taken over for the party to continue. It's a big place so there was plenty of room for everyone. Live Aid was still going on in the USA and the club had put up giant screens so we could watch the bands, live interviews and partying over there.

Once at Legends, everyone started to party *seriously* — and I came down from fairyland with a bump. Rick had paced himself well all day — not a drop before he went on stage and it had been a long day. Once we hit Legends he attacked the booze with a vengeance.

Kevin Godley, who used to be in 10cc, was there so I spent a lot of time talking to him. I'd met his wife Sue the week before and we got on like a house on fire, so it was great to see them again. Kevin had started doing videos for all sorts of people then — Duran Duran, McCartney, Queen — and he and Sue lived in Keith Moon's old house in Chertsey. When Keith moved out he left a Rolls Royce at the bottom of the pool! Everyone liked Keith Moon, but to be honest I didn't when I first met him with Rick in a studio back in Pye days; he kept coming up and squeezing my boobs really hard!

Laughing All Over The World

Kevin had managed to prop Rick up against a wall but, in slow motion, he was slowly falling down it.

'Perhaps you ought to take him home,' said Kevin.

Home? I didn't want to go home. I was savouring every minute of this amazing day.

Rick was talking to the Godleys, and then he started chatting with Justin Hayward of the Moody Blues.

Marie, Justin's wife, wasn't there, so Justin was having a right old moan about how she bossed him around and wore the pants at home. He'd had enough, he said, but then he'd been threatening to leave Marie for years.

'I'm not bloody going home yet. I'll bloody go home when I want!'

But Justin hadn't really chosen the right moment for a heart-to-heart with Rick.

'Right mate,' said Rick as he slumped a little further down the wall and then managed to prop himself up again. 'Yeah, right, man, umm ...' Slide down ... prop up again.

The trouble with these guys is they act like poor little rich boys. Most of them are amazingly egotistical. The deal is: You worship me, you look after me, you let me do what I like. You give *me* children and *I'll* give you money and a name. Women's liberation hasn't hit the rock world — neither has political correctness, believe me!

I couldn't be bothered with Rick and Justin, so I decided to go to the loo. Rick was sliding up and down the wall. It was no good — I'd have to get him home soon.

A car had been ordered to come round the front. On the way up from the ladies' loo I was accosted by some chap who was blocking the stairs.

'Excuse me.'

'Not until you give me a kiss.'

Before I knew what was happening, he'd grabbed me and, as he did, he accidentally pushed me down the stairs.

He didn't mean to hurt me, but I was pretty pissed off. I'd ruined my posh tights, I was worried I'd damaged my lovely

Patty Parfitt

dress and my knee hurt like hell. And there was no carpet on the stairs so I felt a bit shocked for a moment.

Just then Kevin Godley came up.

'Christ, Patty! Are you OK?'

'Yes. No problem. But this bloody idiot is annoying me.'

Kevin turned to the culprit. 'Andrew, calm down and apologise.'

Andrew Ridgely — so that's who he was — looked sheepish and apologised.

'I'm sorry,' he said. 'Sorry, sorry, sorry. I'm a bit pissed.'

Andrew and I made up and as I left I saw him slithering down the wall, too. Little boys! Fortunately Rick had stopped that and was waiting in the foyer for me, swaying, and, together, I limped and he staggered out to the car.

'You took long enough in the loo,' he said.

'This guy Andrew Ridgely was blocking the stairs and I couldn't get past. He wanted me to kiss him.'

Rick turned. 'Right, I'll fucking kill him.'

'No, let's get in the car.' I swivelled him round which is really quite easy when he's totally pissed.

We'd managed to get a few tickets for a couple of guys from the Raven — although everyone had to pay, of course. When they saw us leaving they leapt in the limo with us to cadge a lift home.

Then Rick discovered the champagne in the limo. And it really did help my knee. I'd done my best to pace myself during the day but I think the champagne wasn't the best idea.

By the time we got to Battersea, I felt almost as pissed as Rick although I'd been drinking lemonade for some of the time. Same bubbles – less effect – I did that quite often.

Rick, on the other hand, had woken up. He wanted to carry on, so we all went down to a club we knew near to the flat to see if they were open, but they weren't so we all went home.

That was the first time I actually saw Rick do coke. He'd probably been doing it all night, but I was very naïve then.

I went to the loo and came out and Rick was in the spare

room doing something with some white powder.

'Coke,' he said.

'I thought it was brown.'

Rick thought that was hilarious.

'Don't be a silly cow!'

'Why are you putting it up your nose?'

'What do you expect me to do — put it up my arse?'

'I thought you ate it!'

Rick was in stitches. He went in and told everyone what I'd said and they all fell about.

So then we stayed up for another three or four hours and had a great time. I didn't try coke — not then. I was high enough already. But it was a great party. We only slept for a few hours and woke up feeling great.

And that was really the beginning of the party. Our party.

11

Going Down Town Tonight

Once Rick had decided that I was going to stay he began to woo me to be his housekeeper and mother. He thought he was a dying man. The booze and coke made him feel good, but when he was coming down he felt like shit. He was on his own, the band appeared to have broken up and he was frightened.

'Please stay and look after me,' he used to say regularly. 'Stay. Look after me, I've got no one, for the first time I'm on my own.'

He said it again and again but he didn't need to. I'd always loved Rick. I'd always wanted him, wanted to marry him, wanted to give him children and a nice home. I was happy. I was in love with him — I suppose I always had been — maybe I always will be. Although now it feels like a curse!

There were snags, of course. We didn't have any money. At least, the accountants were giving him £150 a week —

Patty Parfitt

they'd upped it by £50 — to live on but that went absolutely nowhere the way we were living. Fortunately, I had my money from selling the fashion business but that was only a few grand, and we were going through it pretty quickly. But, of course, we partied anyway! Thank God for Peter Stringfellow!

I wasn't quite sure what had been happening in Rick's love life before my return, but I had a fair idea. I knew he hadn't been faithful to Marietta. He told me about his affair with Debbie Ash and he was obviously cut up when she ended that. Then he told me he'd been going out with a page 3 girl called Debbee Ashby. She was blonde — Rick always had to have a blonde on his arm — and she had big tits although Rick wasn't that keen on those, he's always been a leg man. But he was keen enough to take her to see his Mum. She was only seventeen years old at the time (he was thirty seven) so he told Lil that he was 'helping her with her career'. A likely story — but Lil thought Rick was being very kind and believed every word.

When I moved in with Rick, of course, we went to see Lil. She greeted me like a long-lost daughter. We sat in the kitchen and had a cup of tea. Lil was in a confiding mood.

'You heard what happened with Marietta. And then there have been other girls, too, you know. The last one was that model Debbee Ashby but then you couldn't call her a girlfriend, Patty, because nothing happened there.'

I was amused but I was cross, too. It was ridiculous.

'Lil, get real. Of course it did.'

'It didn't, she was only young, he was just helping her out.'

'Lil, he was sleeping with her.'

'Never!' said Lil. 'My Ricky wouldn't do that, she was too young!'

'He was! You don't think that those boobs could go past without a grab!'

'No,' said Lil.

'Ask him,' I said. She did.

'Well, I didn't like to tell you, Mum, but ...'

She clasped her hands together in horror. 'Oh, Ricky!' She still does that, even though Rick is now nearly fifty. It's usually followed by Lil giving her Ricky a loving look, or a kiss, and you can almost hear everyone else around thinking: 'Oh, grow up, Rick!'

As far as I was concerned Rick had finished with Debbee Ashby, or so he said. He'd been out screwing other girls as well, although Debbee didn't know that. It was a shame for her because she was quite sweet and innocent, and really quite a nice girl.

Then one night Rick and I walked into Bootleggers. She was there and took one look at Rick and burst out crying.

I looked at Rick.

'Why's she still so upset?' I asked him. 'You told her, didn't you?'

He shuffled about a bit, looking shifty, the way men do, and said: 'Well, um, I just didn't phone her.'

He went off to talk to someone and I went over to Debbee. I said to her: 'Debbee, I didn't know anything about Rick having left you like that and I'm really sorry.'

'I've known about you for a long time,' she said. 'He's been talking about you coming back, but he didn't say anything about going back with you.'

'I'm really sorry,' I said.

She was sobbing and I put my arm around her.

'You're so nice, but he's such a bastard.' Eventually I went back to Rick who was looking very sheepish but rather smug at the same time.

Later Debbee went to the papers and I don't blame her. Rick wasn't at all amused.

'Bloody girl! All the help I gave her and that's all the thanks I get!'

'Come on, Rick!' I said.

'It's not funny,' he said, just like a little boy.

Patty Parfitt

Life was good in Battersea, but with little or no work to be involved in, Rick was twitchy. Alan and Rick idly discussed dumping Francis from the band, because he didn't want to work any more.

The band got back together for Live Aid but that was it. Rick wanted to work because he needed the money. Francis wasn't so badly off but he wasn't loaded either. Even so, he wasn't convinced. The *End of the Road* tour, which was supposed to rake in loads of money and set them up for life, just hadn't. Francis wasn't a brilliant investor but he was better than Rick and could afford to pause a little and see what he wanted to do next.

Rick is just hopeless with money and how we would have managed without my earnings from Australia, and a loan from my brother and his wife I don't know. Of course, often we could get things on credit or free simply because Rick was Rick Parfitt. We got into all the clubs free and people like Peter Stringfellow would always give us free champagne because it suited him to have famous faces in his club. He was lovely and remembered his friends.

But the coke was expensive. Rick paid for that out of his pocket money or Ron, Rick's driver, got it for him. Then it would go into the accounts as something like £600 to Nicky Brown (Niki Lauder, as in powder and fast!) for services rendered.

Then Rick would pay Ron whenever a royalties cheque came in. After a while it became obvious that one of us was going to have to do some work. Rick was restless and broody, pissed and coked up a lot of the time, so, of course, it had to be me. I prefer working anyway — I like to keep busy.

I managed to find a job as a manicurist in Streatham. My second client was Madame Cyn — Cynthia Payne, famed for her work as London's most notorious madam and brothel owner.

They'd just finished making the film about her with Julie

Laughing All Over The World

Walters, called *Personal Services*, and Cyn wanted to look her best for the première and all the interviews she'd be doing to promote the film. She was terrific fun and we hit it off right away. She wanted to try false nails, and they looked really good, so she decided to have some done again for the première.

'Have you got a man, dear?' asked Cyn, as I carefully fitted her second nail.

'Yes.'

'And what does he do? And so we got on to Rick.

'Oh him!' said Cyn. 'I used to know his old chauffeur, Jim. Jim used to come to loads of my parties. It's a small world isn't it?'

Rick wasn't amused.

'Jim?! What? He was always disappearing and saying he was ill. And all the time he was at Madame Cyn's parties!'

Rick really hated me working. He didn't like being alone in the flat and I wasn't allowed to tell anyone I was working, even other members of the band, because he was terrified it would get into the papers and reflect badly on him. So it all got very tiring, especially since we were out clubbing every night, and then I had to drag myself up every morning to go and fit false nails.

In the end, after about six weeks, Rick couldn't stand it any longer and I just quit — it was simpler. The atmosphere at home in the flat wasn't great. There was all sorts of squabbling with the band. The tax situation was dire for everyone, and the *End of the Road* tour which was supposed to pay it off, hadn't and everyone was very fraught. Alan was trying to work out where all the money had gone, and Francis didn't like that.

Meanwhile Alan and Rick were still trying to work out how to have Status Quo without Francis. It was like living in the midst of a political campaign.

Francis had decided that he didn't want to work with Alan any more and that put Rick in a bit of a spot. He had to choose between them. Logically there was no choice — Francis and Rick *were* Status Quo — but all sorts of ideas were being floated around in our flat. Alan wanted to call the new band — which would be him and Rick — Quo 2. I said that was corny. If they were going to be together, and they were good enough, they should call themselves something completely different. That went down like a lead balloon.

It was a difficult time. Francis said that he didn't really want to work again — and especially not with Alan. Then Alan rang Francis from the flat: 'Hey! Frame! We've got to do some work. We all need the money. Come on — this is stupid.'

But Francis still said no.

Alan was furious. 'I can't understand why Francis doesn't want to bloody well work.'

Rick and I looked at each other because we were both thinking the same thing: 'No, he doesn't want to work with you.' But neither of us said a thing. We didn't want to hurt Nuff's feelings.

We had a hilarious time making up names for a new band when we'd had too much booze and coke. On the surface it was great fun but Rick knew and I knew that it was never going to happen. But Alan didn't. He really believed that Rick was going to split up with Francis and together they were going to form a new band.

Things got worse and worse as Alan started to make plans to wind up his businesses in Australia. Of all of them Alan was the most canny with money. He and Dayle had bought lots of land and put in money to develop retirement houses on the site.

Alan was also trying to sort out somewhere to live in England and get the kids into English schools. Dayle was packing up all their stuff and I think she was looking forward to coming over to the UK. I would have loved it if she had.

The plan was that Alan would return to Australia, sort

everything out, and then come back and launch the new band with Rick. Rick mooched around the flat looking increasingly sheepish. He knew that it wasn't going to happen but he didn't have the balls to tell Alan that and, when Alan left for the airport, Rick and I knew that it would be the last time we saw him for a long time.

History was repeating itself — Rick and Francis never could bring themselves to face a situation and talk openly and honestly about what they wanted to do.

We had an emotional farewell at the flat. Rick said he couldn't make the airport because he wasn't feeling great. Basically he was suffering from a severe case of guilt. In fact, we were both feeling like shit and knowing that it was going to hit the fan very soon.

Soon Alan started ringing up and Rick simply wouldn't answer the phone. You could hear the answerphone going on and Alan saying: 'Rick, Rick, what's going on, man? Call me back.'

But Rick never did. He couldn't face it.

'Where the hell are you, Rick?' Alan used to say on the answerphone. We felt awful listening to him.

This went on for weeks until Alan managed to get through to Colin Johnson. Poor old Colin — it was left to him to break the news, as usual.

'I'm terribly sorry, Alan, but the boys don't want to work with you any more,' said Colin.

'What the hell are you talking about?' said Alan, incredulous.

'They don't want to work with you. Francis has refused to. And Rick doesn't have much choice — he's really sorry.'

'But I've been winding up everything out here,' said Alan, who was frantic. 'I've been selling things off, putting other things on hold, we're packed and ready to come back to the UK.'

'Well, I'm sorry,' said Colin. 'There's nothing I can do. It's out of my hands now.'

Patty Parfitt

Inevitably Alan phoned Rick again. This time Rick actually spoke to him and said something like: 'I had to weigh up my choices. I'm better off with Francis than I would be with you, because Francis is more famous. Although I like you much more than Francis, I'm going with him because I need the money. I'm really sorry, but I haven't got a choice.'

Alan hung up, and after that he and Rick didn't speak for a couple of years. I felt terrible and so did Rick. It was a cowardly way to behave and, however much he tried to justify it to himself, he knew it, too.

Alan was deeply hurt and, on top of that, he then had financial problems of massive proportions. He'd managed to raise the money to develop the land he'd bought because he was a member of Status Quo and had a good income. But now he was no longer a member of the band and he didn't have that guaranteed income. To make matters even worse, the developer ran off with most of his money without laying a single brick.

It was a terrible time for Alan and Dayle; I think Rick and Francis behaved very badly. I don't think they realised how dumping Alan was going to affect his life. Once the bank heard that Alan was no longer in Status Quo they pulled the plug on him, too.

He and Dayle had a beautiful house opposite the beachfront in Rose Bay, one of Sydney's nicest areas and they had to sell it. The land development was a complete mess, Dayle had just had another baby, and was feeling very vulnerable — for the whole family it was a total nightmare. I think that Francis and Rick should take some responsibility for that.

Dayle started to drink too much and Alan was in a shocking state, trying to sort everything out — he lost just about everything. But they have a very strong marriage and they got through it. They survived and they're definitely happier than anyone else in the band now.

Laughing All Over The World

Alan quickly got another band together in Australia and they had a few number one hits over there. That helped financially and probably helped him ego-wise, too. He deserved it.

But these days he's given up music and he's concentrating on his various business ventures and doing very well. Dayle has got herself together, too, and is very successful as an interior designer. So I'll have a job in Oz if I choose to return. I don't know if Alan will ever forgive Rick and Francis. He still feels very bitter about how they treated him even now.

Rick said to me afterwards: 'I'm not proud of myself — of what I've done — but I have to look after myself.'

I don't know what Francis' feelings were on the subject — he never says anything to anyone. I doubt he cared.

As far as we were concerned, the letters kept coming from the bank, and money was really becoming a problem. Inevitably it wasn't long before Francis, Rick and Andy were back in the studio recording again. The album was *In The Army* and this time they teamed up with the two session musicians Jeff Rich and Rhino Edwards who'd worked with Rick on his *Recorded Delivery* album. Francis came to listen to them in the studio and he and Rick agreed to ask them to join Quo. Rhino and Jeff jumped at the chance.

In many ways they fitted in well with the band. Rhino at least smokes dope a lot and does the odd bit of cocaine although nowhere near as much as Francis and Rick.

Jeff was nice, he didn't do drugs, barely drank and hated cigarettes. In the last couple of years I have heard that he's developed a liking for grass and has started smoking a lot. I was really surprised when I heard that.

Andrew and Rhino have always been the most politically minded of the band. They're the only ones who'd ever have a conversation about political issues and who ever went to college, so they thought they were a little intellectually superior to the rest. The others used to call them The

Patty Parfitt

Walkmen because on tour, when they reached a famous city, instead of chilling out at the hotel, they'd get their walking boots on and have a walk around the place sightseeing, visiting the museums and monuments and checking out the best restaurants — and where you could buy the best dope!

Of course, nobody recognised them — the only members of Quo who are recognised are Rick and Francis which is a bit odd when you consider that Andrew, for example, has been with the band for well over 20 years. Rick used to say that Andrew, Jeff and Rhino were a bit low in the personality stakes and behind their backs he always called them the Session Men.

So there was Rick, Francis, Andrew, Jeff and Rhino. The song 'In The Army' got to number two in the charts and everyone was a bit pissed off about that — the only reason it didn't get to number one was because Nick Berry, who was then in the soap *EastEnders*, had recorded a song and had the top spot.

But it was a great boost for Quo. Rick hates not working and a hit was just what he needed.

The band went off and played in the Middle East, in Bahrain and Dubai. They could do warm-up concerts there — it was a kind of testing ground where they could identify any mistakes or weak spots in the set. They also filmed a couple of videos there, 'Rollin' Home' — Rick's first time in a pool since Heidi's death.

Then I'd stay at home while Rick was off. I had a well-earned rest, although I always missed him a lot, and once they came home life seemed to get back to its normal hectic routine of booze and coke and too many evenings out. Rick was still a bit twitchy but we were getting on well. I let things ride a bit. Sometimes he'd get too drunk or too coked up and every now and then he'd throw a punch at me. But he'd never remember it the next day — and he'd go out and buy me some roses to conceal his guilt.

Laughing All Over The World

But the taxman was on his back for half a million, he had no driving licence and he still didn't own his own property, so if you add that all together he was under a lot of stress at the time. Anyway I loved him, so I took it all.

Rick was also worried about how the fans would take to the new Quo. Would they like the new line-up and sound? They planned a tour of the provinces to test the waters.

My parents were living in Swindon so I joined the band there for the first gig and all the family came along. And Quo went down brilliantly.

Francis and Rick were getting on OK but for both of them it was a difficult time. Behind the scenes there were all kinds of arguments — mainly about money. Colin Johnson was going through a divorce from his American wife Helene so Alan Crux, who had been the accountant, took over as manager for a time while Colin sorted out his personal problems.

When we were still at Valiant House in 1986, everyone involved in the music side of The Prince's Trust was invited for drinks with Charles and Diana at Kensington Palace. Quo did the first concert for the Trust so obviously they were on the guest list — at least there was Francis, Rick and me, Colin Johnson and a management guy called Steve and his wife. Rick and I had a Rolls Royce and I drove. Steve and his wife met us at Valiant House.

Rick had bought me some beautiful diamond and pearl earrings which he was going to give to me at Christmas but he presented them to me early especially for the occasion.

I bought a black velvet Terence Hodler dress and some black Charles Jourdan shoes from Diana's favourite shoe shop, Russell and Bromley in Knightsbridge. She'd been the day before for some herself, the shop assistant told us. Rick looked great in his shiny blue raw silk suit.

The party was fun, all very civilised. We sipped champagne and just soaked up the atmosphere — it was hard to believe we were really there. Charles and Diana

Patty Parfitt

both nodded at us but Steve, instead of introducing Rick to the Prince and Princess, introduced us to some band he'd just signed and was trying to get a record deal for. They hadn't even released a single.

Rick and Francis were furious. But it got worse. Suddenly we heard Steve having a very loud, effing and blinding row with Colin, Quo's manager. Prince Charles turned round to stare at them, then diplomatically ignored them. We were really embarrassed.

'Christ,' said Rick. 'Steve's been doing coke in the loo!'

'What? Here?!'

'Yeah. That's it, we're leaving. That is well out of order! We're not taking him back with us. I don't want people to even know that we know him. We'll take his wife but not him.'

In fact, she didn't want to come with us — she decided to stay with Steve — so we went home and then to The Raven, which was a bit of a come-down after Kensington Palace. We were both furious that Steve had spoiled everyone's evening.

Alan was still there in the background asking where all the money had gone. But he, together with Ian Jones, who was road manager at the time, did get things moving.

The band went off to play a few gigs in Russia and I don't know how the finances worked but afterwards one of the management would turn up with paper bags full of thousands of pounds in cash.

Rick and I moved to a lovely flat, Rick had a property of his own at last. It was small but with a lovely view — overlooking the Thames at Teddington and we'd hardly moved in before one of the management turned up with a carrier bag stuffed full of £50 and £20 notes.

He called everyone 'Kid', including Rick which infuriated him. But Rick would bite his lip when he turned up with cash.

'Stash this somewhere, Kid,' he would say.

Laughing All Over The World

At one time I had £15,000 in a carrier bag stuffed behind the fridge in the flat!

Alan Lancaster wasn't happy when he read about the band's new single, album and tour. He believed that since he had started the band in the first place, he should keep the name Status Quo. His money problems were still horrendous but Rick and Francis were determined to keep the name and after a court battle they won. Rick and Francis *were* Status Quo.

Many of the fans identify with Rick because he's one of the lads, he's charming and fun. But on stage Francis still has that edge even though Rick is the better singer. And the singer is supposed to be the most famous one — at least usually.

When people talk about Status Quo they always talk about Francis Rossi and Rick Parfitt.

Rick thinks Francis is sly and I think he's right. Francis is shrewd. Rick always called him The Sly Fox but when I wrote that once in a letter — something like 'You and your sly fox'. Rick kept the letter but crossed out 'sly fox'. He was terrified of anyone seeing it written down.

He's not frightened of Francis — he knows Francis wouldn't drop him, because Status Quo is the two of them together. But Rick's Cousin Sue claims that Francis can't wait for the day when he's rich enough to walk away from Quo again.

Then he wouldn't have to put up with Rick's tantrums any more. When he talked of Rick to Cousin Sue he always referred to him as 'your fucking cousin.'

But there's a bond between them, although that doesn't mean they like each other.

Rick is flamboyant and likes clothes — Francis couldn't give a shit about what he wears and it shows. He will dress up because he has to but he'd much rather be in a tracksuit or jeans. And he wouldn't dream of wearing jeans out. Rick once said in an interview that he had 120 pairs of jeans. Fibber! He had about four to six pairs at my last count!

Patty Parfitt

At one time he did have eight but we used two of them to patch the other six!

We never saw Francis socially, which is amazing when you think about it. The only time we saw him was when he and Rick were working together, or had to attend some kind of function. Then everybody sits at the same table and pretends they like each other. It was total hypocrisy.

Rick's a joker but Francis gets sick of his jokes. 'I'm sick to death of hearing Rick's jokes again and again,' he'd say. And he was sick of Rick getting out of it and throwing up all the time. Although, let's face it, Francis is hardly squeaky clean. When Francis gets out of it, it's usually because he's smoked some dope — he smokes almost non-stop — and then he just sits there and smiles to himself. He doesn't actually say anything — it's as if he's having a private joke with himself.

Francis used to get very cross when Rick lost control. Rick would often fall over. That annoyed Francis and, sometimes when Rick had been boozing, he'd oversleep and miss a recording in the morning. That used to drive Francis mad because they had to keep the studio open and it cost thousands of pounds.

Sometimes Rick was so bad he couldn't sing his words properly. If he had a bad hangover or if he'd been smoking cigarettes heavily the night before, it would affect his voice and he couldn't reach the high notes, his voice would crack. It was more money wasted — frowns all round.

When things like that started going wrong in the studio or at rehearsal, Rick and Francis would have terrible screaming matches and, although the fans would see Rick and Francis getting on well on stage, in fact, the rows used to continue out front as well. It was the usual thing. Rick loves playing really loud but because he's rhythm he can drown everyone else out. So Francis would shout at him to turn the amp down. Marshall Amps actually made him an amp that goes up to 13 — they actually stop at 12. He loves that.

Laughing All Over The World

On videos you can see Francis and Rick grinning at each other and laughing together. In fact, what Rossi is really saying is: 'Turn that fucking thing down!' Then, when Rick won't, he goes and turns it down himself. Just to annoy Francis, Rick grins and goes and turns it up again.

If Francis really wants to annoy Rick he'll simply ignore him. Rick is bursting for a fight and Francis just refuses to listen to him. That drives Rick mad. The other way is to take the piss out of him.

It was a standing joke that Rick expected everything to be done for him and Francis was constantly saying to Cousin Sue, the dresser or the other wardrobe ladies: 'He's like a baby — he needs feeding and changing. He needs his bum wiped.'

The other thing that Francis didn't like about Rick was the way he talked to people. I know Rick treated Marietta like dirt, sometimes in front of other people and she didn't deserve that. Rick embarrassed her publicly. Francis' love life has been complicated, and he's certainly been no angel where women are concerned, but he wouldn't humiliate a woman in public.

But Rick never did that to me. If he was going to be foul to me, he'd do it in the privacy of our own home. It was always private between us.

He was always very nice to me in front of the band because he wanted them to know that we were so happy, and adored each other. In fact, it was true — Rick was only horrible when he'd drunk too much whisky or done too much coke.

What he was really saying was: 'Our relationship is wonderful — yours are crap!' It was the old rivalry thing again.

I got on well with the rest of the band. Jeff, the drummer, was in total awe of Francis and was always hanging around him which pissed Rick off. The rest of the band used to joke about it — they joke about everything. 'Oh, Jeff's up

Patty Parfitt

Francis' bum again!' they'd say and poor Jeff was always quoting Francis, too. Francis pretends not to enjoy the attention but he does like being the Man. He's always very cool. He doesn't want people thinking that he's a show off or anything. But if you don't pay attention to Francis, he doesn't like it. He rarely opens up but I remember once we were both lying by a swimming pool in Nassau and, for a change, Francis started to talk. There were two other girls there and they were asking him: 'Didn't you miss not being on the road?'

It was a question most of us dare not ask. But, for once, Francis was prepared to answer.

'Yeah,' he said. 'I did miss it. I missed the money and I missed being *him* — Francis Rossi the rock star. But I don't like having to do all the interviews and all that crap and going out to dinner. But I like being on stage and I like being him — Francis Rossi — and then I like taking my wig off and going home and doing the garden and checking on the Koi carp.'

And that sums him up. He likes to be private and keep his women at home under lock and key. In many ways he leads a double life. There's Francis Rossi, the rock star, and Francis Rossi, the family man who still had his mum living with him, until she died quite recently, a man who likes doing his garden.

Rick is the complete opposite. He loves being a non-stop star. I suppose it was inevitable, with all the attention, that he has changed.

I always called him Ricky, just like his Mum. To me he always was Ricky, the boy I met when I was seventeen. Rick is someone different. Rick is that chap from Status Quo — Rick Parfitt, someone very different, someone not very nice at times. It's sad but Ricky died a long time ago. Sometimes he comes back — usually when times are hard — but as soon as the money comes in again Ricky dies and Rick Parfitt of Status Quo takes over.

them to bits and they go away happy, with lots of quotes. But as soon as they've gone he'll say: 'Fat stupid old cow!' or 'Stupid bitch! Her legs are disgusting!' or 'What a prat that bloke was!' and he'll talk to his PR people and say: 'Don't get him or her again!'

I didn't like it — but I loved him and I didn't want to lose him. Besides, we wanted children. We'd only known each other twenty years so it was about time!

12

What You're Proposing

Come 1988 we were very settled and happy. It was ironic because everyone else seemed to be going through traumas of massive proportions.

Despite having had a beautiful daughter, Bernadette, with the lovely Irish girl, Liz, Francis had dumped her for a stunning Indian girl called Paige, the daughter of a rich jeweller in Manchester, who he met when the band were playing a gig up there. She, in turn, had been dumped for Eileen, now Francis' second wife. Francis had known Eileen for years. She taught music to the deaf and dumb in New York and was a good friend of his cousin Patrick who lived there. Occasionally Francis would pop over and see Patrick and, often, he'd meet Eileen, too. Then, on one visit, Eileen confessed to Francis that her husband was beating her up. She was terrified and wanted to get away but didn't know where to go.

Francis told her to get her bags and come back to England and live with him. He'd marry her, he said.

Patty Parfitt

As well as the readjustments to his love life, Francis also had to accept the fact that his son, Simon, was gay. Francis went public and told the *Daily Mirror* it was his 'proudest moment' when Simon had told him.

Colin was off work, trying to sort his domestic problems with Helene, and he paid a heavy price for it.

There had already been arguments and bickering behind the scenes. *In The Army* was the last album Colin worked on with Quo. Francis wanted one particular song to be the first single from the album because he'd promised his then girlfriend Paige that it would be. Colin, who'd always chosen singles from the albums successfully, disagreed. He said it should be 'In The Army'. He and Francis argued. Colin won but it did nothing for their relationship.

There was plenty of squabbling and, in Colin's absence, people who wanted a change of management began to stir things up. Colin was being slagged off on all sides. If enough mud is thrown, some is bound to stick. Rick and Francis listened to the mud slingers and decided that Colin would have to go. They didn't have the balls to tell him themselves, as usual, so they got Alan Crux to do it.

Colin, embroiled in a vicious divorce which was costing him a fortune, was devastated but resigned. Financially it was a severe body blow, but all the arguments had been getting him down. In the early days it had been hard work but good fun; the band had a laugh, but they were professional and kept things in perspective. Now, probably because they were all worried about money, it wasn't fun any more; they were taking themselves too seriously and everyone was bitching about everyone else. He'd had a good innings and, anyway, he felt Quo's music wasn't going anywhere.

Colin accepted his fate and, his divorce finalised, he pondered what to do next. Even so, he was confused about why he actually got the sack.

He once asked Rick: 'So why the sudden rift? What happened?'

Rick was uncomfortable. 'Well, one of the reasons was that you wanted us to do the *Des O'Connor Show*.'

Colin almost found it funny. He said: 'First I wouldn't accept a show without discussing it with you and secondly I wouldn't put you on that anyway!'

Six months after Colin's departure Quo appeared on the *Des O'Connor Show*!

Alan in Australia was still panicking about money — where had it all gone? Some people told Rick and Francis that Colin had been squirreling away his own tidy little pile without their knowledge.

Rick appeared on his friend Chris Tarrant's show and accused Colin of stealing £8 million from the band. He later said it was £2 million, then £1 million … Furious, Colin Johnson got the figures together with the accountant who had worked on them and sent the whole lot over to Quo's new office. After that nothing more was said.

But one night in Morton's, Mayfair, the two came face to face. Colin wasn't prepared to let the matter rest.

He pulled Rick aside.

'What the fuck was all that about?'

'I don't want to talk about that now, man,' said Rick moving away.

'Well, I do. What was it all about?'

'Oh, we were just told that that's what you'd done …'

'Well, you're a fucking idiot to have believed that crap!'

And fortunately the matter petered out.

Alan Crux and Ian Jones were still in charge, but Francis and Rick were impressed by a manager called David Walker, who had managed several big bands, including Mud and Sweet and also managed Pip Williams who was Quo's producer at the time. They got on well with Walker, they thought he was a great bloke, and he was really keen to manage Quo, too.

The trouble was — what about Crux and Jones?

Pretty soon the mud started flying again, the band fired Alan

Patty Parfitt

Crux and David Walker became manager. Soon Ian Jones was on the way out, too.

But he wasn't the last of the old team to go.

Faithful Ron Brown was told that he wasn't allowed to talk to his friend Colin again. Ron was used to doing as he was told by the band but he had a stubborn streak, and refused to dump a friend on orders.

So he left, too. Management told Rick that we were not to have any further contact with Ron. To make matters worse Ron had already had one heart attack and a heart by-pass operation — and he still wasn't right. He went on to have two dozen more operations. In fact, Ron is very ill now. He is on massive doses of morphine, and the doctors say he will be gone within days. As this book goes to press, Harry and I are staying with him, saying our goodbyes.

Rick missed his old friend and he hated all the fighting. As usual, he always tried to avoid difficult situations; he had to think of number one. Everyone loved Rick, and for good reason, but most people would agree that if you dangled a carrot big enough in front of him he'd do just about anything you said.

*   *   *

Rick and I never talked about marriage. It was almost as if we'd been through all that before. We'd met, fallen in love, and got engaged all those years ago. Then it had all fallen apart. Now we were back together but I didn't want to jeopardise all that. So I never said a thing and he didn't either. It was just kind of assumed that we'd stay together.

Of course, the papers cottoned on that we were back together and Rick was always quoted as saying: 'Patty knows I won't marry her but we both want children.'

Even so, it was a surprise when he proposed again. And again. As the months passed I think he proposed eight times in all and every time I said no. Yes, I loved him, yes, I wanted to marry him, but I wanted to marry him under the right conditions.

Every time I said no he said: 'Okay, I understand but you *will* say yes in the end — I'll just keep asking you.'

When we were still in the flat in Battersea, Rick and the band had gone to Dubai and he came back with a ring for me. It was beautiful, gold with five diamonds. I was thrilled, but was it an eternity ring, an engagement ring or what? Which finger should I put it on?

'It's an engagement ring, Patty, you know what finger that goes on.'

I just took it out of its box and looked at it not knowing what to do.

'Let's talk about getting married,' he said.

'When the time is right, I'd love to, but I don't think you're ready and I'd rather it be right than get a divorce.'

'OK,' he said. 'But take the ring.' And he put it on the wedding finger of my left hand. As Paige later informed me the ring was actually a half eternity ring. Perhaps this was a sign that we'd only have half an eternity together. How true!

Then, when we were in the new flat in Teddington, Quay West, he went to Germany to do promotions for the new Quo and came back with two rings — a wedding and engagement ring with five diamonds. For himself.

'I got bored — so I bought a wedding and engagement ring,' he said, showing off a white gold wedding ring with gold at its centre and a half-eternity ring in white gold with five diamonds, which he proudly displayed on his left hand. 'Oooh,' I said, 'I think you usually buy the girl the wedding ring first.'

But Rick liked to do things differently.

Then he was off to do rehearsals for the 1988 British tour.

'When I come back from rehearsals I think we should discuss it again.'

I was holding off because he wasn't quite together, he was

Patty Parfitt

doing a lot of coke at the time. I just said: 'OK, go and we'll talk about it when you get back.'

We were happy together, especially when we moved to the new flat in Teddington. We were very close then and Rick was feeling good. He was working again and that always makes him feel good. There was a lot happening, they were getting the new band together and recording *In The Army* down in Chipping Norton.

I'd go and stay down there with him for a few days and then come home and he'd join me when he could. It was good and close and warm. The marriage thing hadn't been settled. We had our rings but we didn't really talk seriously about the future. Perhaps we were both afraid to.

I think Rick was faithful to me when we were living together, I like to think so. Of course, rumours reached me that he wasn't.

When Rick was at home he liked to play backgammon. He taught me how to play and I was getting quite good at it. One night we sat down and he said : 'Right, this is serious. If you beat me at backgammon, and I really mean it, we must get married.'

I laughed. 'No, you'll just let me win.'

'No way,' he laughed. 'Besides you know the game too well by now and you'd know if I was letting you win.'

So we sat opposite each other, lined up a couple of glasses of wine and battle commenced.

It was all very civilised and he was really trying. So was I! I thought: 'Right, Ricky Parfitt, I'm going to thrash you and you won't like it because I'll *really* thrash you!'

I won the first game.

Rick won the second. Shit!

Tension mounts and we're both concentrating like mad.

The bastard — there was no way he was going to win this one! And, hallelujah, I thrashed him!

Later he used to joke that he'd let me win but I said: 'No, you didn't. Don't be a bad loser, I actually did beat you!'

Laughing All Over The World

So then he went down on one knee and asked me to marry him and I said yes. I was actually in control for once — the only time it seems!

Later the papers asked if he'd actually gone down on one knee and he said no.

I said: 'Yes, you did.'

'I know I did,' said Rick. 'But I'm not telling them that!'

It was June and we decided to get married in July. The band were so busy it was a question of fitting everything into the schedule. There was two weeks to get everything ready for the wedding and there was no way Rick was going to organise it. Having proposed and got a result the rest was obviously down to me.

'Right then, girl, you go and sort out the register office and all that,' he said and then the ball was in my court.

He was recording in Chipping Norton, so I did everything. Two days before the wedding I suddenly remembered something I'd forgotten — my wedding ring. Rick already had his, so I said: 'I don't like to ask but you know you've got your wedding ring, well, I haven't got one.'

'Oh yeah,' said Rick. 'Well, just go out and buy one.'

So I did. I visited a jewellers in Teddington and got one like Rick's — white and yellow gold except his was yellow gold on the outside with white in the middle and mine was the other way around.

Rick was strange about the wedding. He talked of little else — apart from what the band were doing, of course — but he didn't want anyone to know about it. I travelled down to Chipping Norton where the band were working and told Rick: 'These are the dates the register office can do, so decide because we've got to let Mum and Dad know and everything.'

He said: 'We don't want anyone there — just us.'

I was devastated. This was going to be the biggest day of my life — I wanted my Mum, Dad and family there, and I was sure that he'd want his parents there, too.

'But we've got to have the Mums and Dads.'

'No,' he said. 'No one comes.'

Patty Parfitt

I was upset so the next day he said: 'OK, just the Mums and Dads.'

'What about my sister and brother?'

'No, just the Mums and Dads.'

I searched high and low for a dress. My Mum got married in a dark navy dress and that picture kind of stayed in my mind. I looked everywhere and I couldn't find anything I liked. Then suddenly in the Kensington Hyper Hyper there was this black dress with lace. I thought: 'I'm going to buy that because I love it!' but I can't wear that for the wedding.

So I got it but no other dress seemed to match up to it — so that was it: I'd get married in black! The big black hat came from John Lewis and the flowers were from the local florist. I got some nice carnations for our parents' button-holes and Rick. I was quite pleased with myself for getting everything so organised in such a rush.

Rick was adamant that he didn't want to tell anyone, especially the band about what was going on. On the night before the wedding the band were playing the Brighton Conference Centre so I went down there and Rick and I spent most of the time in huddles in the corner discussing wedding plans — very rock 'n' roll, I don't think.

The rest of the band obviously had their suspicions that something was going on but no one said anything. I was in and out of the dressing room to see Rick and then it was nearly time to go on stage so I popped in and Francis was there playing guitar. Suddenly he broke into playing 'The Wedding March'. I blushed.

'Sorry,' said Frame grinning. 'Wrong tune!'

'What a stupid song to play, Francis!'

'Yes, Miss B. Or is it Mrs P?'

'What are you going on about? You're all giggling like little boys in a corner — stupid as usual!'

They all laughed and I stomped off feeling a fool — and terribly nervous for some reason I can't really quite understand even now.

I watched the gig which went well and Rick and I met up afterwards. We stayed the night in Brighton but we had to get back to London early for the wedding which was planned for 2.30pm.

'Look,' Rick said, 'I know you would have wanted a big wedding but I just couldn't face it — not after last time.'

He and Marietta had been married in Woking Register Office but after that they'd gone to Germany and done the whole bit for her family, a Catholic white wedding and all that went with it and Rick said he absolutely hated it. It wasn't him. He didn't feel comfortable at all.

Rick and I had a Rolls Royce at the time, a Silver Shadow, so, since he was banned, I drove us back in that in the morning. We stopped for a livening drink at The Bear in Oxshott and then went to the flat and got all togged up. We'd arranged for a limo to pick up my Mum and Dad from Swindon, and his Mum and Dad from Woking, and I thought we might get a driver to take us to the register office. But not a bit of it. 'You can drive,' said Rick.

So there I was driving us to our wedding in the Rolls wearing a huge hat which kept hitting the doors and the roof and Rick on the nose, and all the drivers were thinking silly bitch because I really could hardly see where I was going. Plus I was wearing my shades — that, at least, was very rock 'n' roll!

We stopped at an off-licence and got two miniatures each of vodka and tonic, drank them, then headed for Richmond Registry Office.

I took my Polaroid camera because we hadn't ordered a photographer — he wanted to keep it all very quiet — but when we arrived I managed to pin carnations on the Mums and Dads. Mum had brought her camera as well, but it was lucky I had mine because Mum is the world's worst photographer — she gets lots of lovely sky and half heads and legs. She never seems to get the middle bits!

It was all quite mad but that was the norm for us, and it was such a special day. We laughed a lot. I don't think Rick and I have ever been happier — except at the birth of our son.

We asked the registrar to take some photos for us and then we walked out into the sunshine. It was a perfect day — except there was a photographer and reporter from the *Sun*.

'How the bloody hell did you know?' said Rick but he wasn't that cross.

'It certainly wasn't me,' I said. If I'd tipped off the press when Rick wanted a quiet day I knew I would have been hanged.

It turned out that Ian Jones had told them, and Rick seemed quite pleased in the end — so we got the front page of the *Sun* and they sent us some lovely pictures which proved it wasn't a dream (or nightmare even!).

I was feeling as happy as I ever have been. I had something old — a beautiful antique bracelet of hers that my Mum had given me which I'd always admired. I had something blue — because Mum bought me a blue garter, and someone lent me a bracelet. The new was yet more white knickers from Rick!

After the ceremony we all went back to what the band have always called 'Tequila Palace'. It's the Sheraton Hotel at Heathrow but they call it that because that's where they all had their first margaritas.

Francis and some of the crew were staying there. Francis was there because of Paige — he couldn't take her home because of his Mum! The crew were staying there because they were playing Wembley the next day. Rhino, Jeff and Andrew lived quite nearby so they were at home.

Francis virtually had a permanent room there. He and Paige always used to have two rooms with interlocking doors. Francis has a thing about bathrooms. He can't share one. He won't share a loo or bath or shower with anyone — that's one of his funny habits. He doesn't like anyone being in his bathroom or sitting on his loo!

On tour, it apparently cost a fortune because if he has a woman with him, they have to have two rooms or suites so that the girl has got her own bathroom and doesn't have to darken the door of Francis'. He simply likes a room to do his ablutions on his own and heaven only knows what he gets up to in there! I think perhaps he's got a bit of a phobia about hygiene and cleanliness.

At the hotel, we were shown to our room and we gasped — it was a fantastic suite.

'But I didn't order this,' Rick said and it turned out it was a present from the band — paid for by the band so Rick ended up paying for a share of it anyway!

Room service laid on a buffet in the suite for us which was really nice and we had a very happy party before the Mums and Dads went off. The rest of the band hadn't arrived — just Francis, Paige and Paul the minder — they wouldn't go anywhere without a minder to carry the bags and be on hand in case they got into trouble with the hotel, which they often did.

With our parents' congratulations echoing down the corridor we retreated back to the suite and Francis phoned.

'I told you you were getting married,' he said.

'I know,' I laughed, 'but I'm not telling you anything! Are you going to come in for a drink?'

'We'll pop down later,' said Paige.

They were only down the corridor but they never showed up. Paige told me later that Francis didn't want to join us and party — you know what he's like. She was disappointed, she wanted to come and celebrate but we knew what Francis was like. We didn't care. I hadn't had much to drink but I felt on a real high, I was as high as a kite just on the excitement of getting married.

I'd always known in my heart that Ricky and I would be married one day and here I was — Mrs Parfitt!

Rick was really happy. He couldn't stop smiling. When the registrar declared us man and wife he'd turned to me and said: 'We did it then.'

I said: 'Yep. It took bloody long enough, didn't it?'

Patty Parfitt

'But I always told you we'd do it.'

'Yeah, we've always known that, everyone has.'

'All this for this,' he said. 'Well, here we are — hello missus!'

At the hotel the smile never left his face.

'This is so different from my last marriage,' he said. 'I'm actually enjoying this one! The other one was a pain in the arse and I kept on going to the loo and having a smoke and doing drugs. This is totally different though, this is lovely.'

'Can I phone a few people and tell them?'

'Yeah, why not?'

So I hit the phone. I called my brother and sister and the Godleys. They went mad.

Later the biggest arrangement of flowers you've ever seen in your life arrived in the suite from the Godleys. Sue, Kevin's wife, stood over the florist and told her exactly what she wanted. Other flowers arrived from management and the band and then we went down to dinner, to Lily's Bar and Grill where they have a cabaret. It was all great fun.

They told everyone that we'd just got married and I was getting brandies sent over to me left right and centre, from the management, and from the guests. I don't drink brandy but I thought — sod it! Afterwards the Tiller Girls got me up on stage with them, doing a can can and making a right arse of myself.

It was a wonderful evening and we both got thoroughly pissed — there was no coke at all that night. Finally Rick helped me back up to the suite. He was OK — he could handle it better than me. I suppose his body was more used to it. But I was gone, totally gone.

I sat down on the plush satin-covered sofa and looked at the bowls of fruit and pot pourri on the glass coffee table. Oh God. Oh no. Rick moved the pot pourri just in time, but I was sick all over the fruit. Rick was wonderful — he cleared it up and flushed it down the loo, fruit and all.

'You feel better now?' he said.

I think I said: 'Yes,' then ... I was sick again — in the pot pourri.

Rick seemed to find it all very funny and flushed it down the loo. I was terrible. I really threw my heart up.

'We're allowed to be sick. We've just got married, darlin'. It doesn't matter. I'm going to see everything about you. It's all right,' said Rick, pissed as a rat himself, but somehow managing much better than me.

Sick again!

'That's fine, go on dear.'

'I'm going to die.'

'No, you're not. Trust me.'

So this was married bliss — Status Quo style! A honeymoon night of passion — you've got to be joking! We both fell on the bed and passed out.

The following day the band were playing Wembley. Rick let me lie in. By the time he came back to wake me up he'd already been downstairs and had coffee with Paul, a guy from the road crew.

My eyes seemed stuck together but once I'd come to I didn't feel too bad — considering how bad I should have felt.

Rick sat on the bed.

'Good morning, Mrs P. Look — we're in the papers.'

'Oh God — no!' Back under the duvet. Then I opened half an eye and there we were on the front page of the *Sun*.

'Come on, get up, we've got to go.'

'I've got to have a shower, Rick.'

Quick kiss on the cheek. 'Make it quick.'

Once I'd showered and put on some make-up I felt fine. In fact I felt good. No hangover whatsoever. I suppose the brandy had gone with the fruit and pot pourri and I was still on a high from getting married.

We went straight from the hotel to Wembley to do a sound check and then went backstage to wait for the gig.

I wore my wedding dress and we had a great party — it really was like our wedding reception. Rick liked it — he didn't have to pay for it!

Patty Parfitt

I stayed on the side of the stage while the band played. Rick liked me to be where he could see me. He wanted to make sure I wasn't wandering off or talking to another man so I was always there for him in the wings. Sometimes Paige stood with me.

When Quo went on stage, Francis told the fans that we'd just got married. 'I suppose we'll have to call him Mr Parfitt now,' he said and the whole audience cheered and shouted congratulations. Rick took a bow.

'That's enough,' said Francis. 'It's going to his head. This is obviously not our gig — it's his. Fair enough, he can have this one. And her over there,' he went on, pointing at me. 'Come over here.'

One of the road crew tried to push me on stage but I was going: 'No! No! No!'

With hindsight I wish I'd gone on stage but I was too nervous and embarrassed. So I ran downstairs and locked myself in the loo!

Rick later said that he'd have liked me to have thrown my bouquet to the fans but it didn't happen.

He always wanted me to stand in the wings looking at him adoringly. Sometimes he'd ask me to go around to the front of house and see what it sounded like and what reaction they were getting from the fans. Then I could report back later and say things like: 'They didn't like that song — that's the one where lots of people went to get a drink' or 'That's a low time and they get a bit restless then. So you need to go straight back onto a fast number.'

Quo like to keep their audience on a high all the time, they don't like to give them a chance to slow down. But most of the time Rick just wanted me there, for moral support I suppose.

The Wembley gig was great — one of the best they'd done. They had another the next day and that was great, too. It was the last gig of the tour and afterwards we went off to Stringfellows to celebrate our wedding, me in white this time.

Of course, Francis wouldn't come — you have to drag him kicking and screaming into any nightclub — and it wasn't a proper wedding reception, just a few friends for drinks — like Mike Winters, Mike Macgear, Paul McCartney's brother, and an assortment of others, and, of course, Peter Stringfellow, who introduced me to B and B — Bollinger and Bristol (champagne and sherry).

It was terrific fun, and then Rick and I went back to our flat at Quay West and carried on partying until four or five in the morning, by which time we were so pissed we just fell into bed and passed out.

I'd always felt 'married' to Status Quo in a funny kind of way. Now it was official. God help me!

13

Fun, Fun, Fun

Before we got married, we were trying for a baby which turned out not to be as simple as I had anticipated. In fact, we had been trying in a lackadaisical kind of way for ages — in other words, we weren't using any protection and we sort of hoped that nature would take its course. But three years on — nothing.

But once married we started *really* trying in earnest.

I tried everything, all the usuals: the sexy underwear, I took my temperature every day and pounced on him when the time was right, I tried arousing potions, everything — but I still couldn't conceive.

The coke and the booze didn't help Rick. Neither did the sleeping tablets, called Rohypnol, which he was addicted to. The band called them donkeys because they could knock a donkey out, no trouble. They frightened me. When he'd taken them he would sleep like a corpse, it was a dead sleep, and I was always checking him to see that he was

Patty Parfitt

actually still breathing and alive. Rick had taken milder tablets like Mogadon before, especially after Heidi died, but these were something else.

Rick got the tablets from his doctor who was a smashing bloke and no fool. Rick went to see him when we were having trouble conceiving and Rick was also having problems getting a good night's sleep.

The doctor told him: 'These are the strongest sleeping tablets around. All you need is half a tablet a night. No more. They are not addictive but they're for short-term use only. You must stick *strictly* to the correct dosage.'

'Right,' said Rick. But the doctor obviously didn't know Rick very well. If Rick wants something he wants it *now*!

So he took the half tablet and because it didn't work instantly he took more. In the end he was taking two or three tablets a night.

Because they didn't work instantly — few tablets do — Rick got into the habit of taking them with him when we went out. If he knew it was going to be a late night and he knew he needed to get some sleep before work the next day, he'd carry them with him and take them in the cab on the way home. Unfortunately sometimes he didn't get the timing right so he'd conk out in the taxi and I'd be left to drag him into the building, shove him in the lift, prop him up over my back and kind of pull him into the flat. I couldn't believe my own strength! Even Rick was amazed!

Now I'm not surprised at the effect the tablets had on Rick. The drug has been in the news recently and has been christened by the newspapers the 'date rape drug'. Some horrible creeps have been slipping it into girls' drinks leaving them powerless to resist attack.

Medically it's used to treat severe back pain — or insomnia. Rick had insomnia but it's probably the worst drug that could have been prescribed for him. Of course, none of this improved our chances of conceiving!

Laughing All Over The World

I went with Rick when he went to see the doctor. I didn't go in, but I sat in the waiting room. The doctor had a loud voice, so has Rick, and the door was very thin — so I managed to hear just about everything.

Doctor: 'Rick, are you doing drugs?'

Rick, with sincerity: 'Oh no, doctor.'

Doctor: 'Are you drinking a lot?'

Rick: 'No, not really — just the usual.' That at least was true — the usual for Rick!

Doctor: 'Are you getting on with Patty OK?'

Rick: 'Oh yes, it's not that. I love Patty and she does everything to try and help me. I couldn't survive without her.'

Then the doctor went on with some suggestions and I jumped over to the other side of the waiting room until Rick came out clutching his sleeping pill prescription.

I had to see the doctor shortly afterwards. I thought long and hard before I saw him and in the end I decided that I really should tell him that Rick was drinking a lot and doing quite a bit of coke. Funnily enough, he wasn't at all surprised.

I was worried that Rick's sex life had been affected by his relationship with Debbie Ash. I know he genuinely cared for her and she dumped him. That was the first time in Rick's life that he'd ever been dumped and he found it very difficult to cope with.

Debbie had got fed up with him being out of it all the time. When he was like that, he couldn't have sex, so she banned him from the bedroom. By the time Rick had said that everything was OK and he'd got it together she didn't want to know. And Rick was pretty broke by this time thanks to his divorce from Marietta and, as Rick's mum said, if not in these words, that didn't really appeal to Debbie.

She chucked him out. He put all his belongings into his Range Rover and went home to Mum for a couple of days but that didn't last long. After that he took up residence in

Patty Parfitt

The Chelsea Hotel in the King's Road — very nice — and he stayed there for six months. I think Debbie really just wanted to end the affair, but the rejection was an enormous blow to Rick.

On reflection I think it was Debbie who got it right — it was me and Marietta who both got it wrong by pandering to his ego. Of course, he walked all over us both.

The doctor told me that perhaps I ought to refuse to have sex with Rick for a few days. But I didn't like that and Rick got really ratty so it didn't work.

In the end it was the singer Gloria Estefan who came to the rescue and, if I ever meet her, I really must thank her. I read an article by her in a magazine in which she said that she and Emilio had had problems conceiving, too, because he had a low sperm count.

I didn't know if Rick had a low sperm count or not — and he point blank refused to be tested. I tried to persuade him by telling him that there would be lots of dirty magazines at the clinic for him to enjoy.

'I'll go for that,' he said. 'But I'm not doing it in a bloody jar! I've had two children — there's nothing wrong with *me*. It must be you.'

But I'd had tests and the doctors said I was fine. Even so I let him blame me. The male ego had to be massaged.

Gloria Estefan said that she got pregnant by standing on her head immediately after making love.

So one day in September, 14 September, to be precise, after Rick and I had made love at Quay West, he went off to make a cup of tea, and I stood on my head. Unfortunately, Gloria didn't specify how long she'd stood on her head so I thought I'd give it as long as I could. 'Bloody hell,' I thought. 'I could be here all day!'

Rick came back with the tea and stood stock still in the doorway.

'What the fuck do you think you're doing?'

'Making a baby.'

'How do you work that out?'

So I told him. He thought it was hilarious and spilt tea all over the carpet. But two days later I knew, I just *knew* that I was pregnant. Rick was thrilled. Me too. So Harry was conceived in that flat and not at sea on our boat, *Silver Sun*, as Rick always likes to claim.

'Let's do a test.'

'We can't yet, we have to wait two weeks.'

Those two weeks crawled by. The test was positive! Rick and I were over the moon. We trotted off to the doctor in Harley Street just to get it confirmed and I came home on cloud nine.

'Tell your Mum first,' said Rick, which I thought was very nice of him. Then we rang round the rest of the family and they were all thrilled, too, although Lil was a bit peeved we told my Mum before her!

But, the baby business apart, life went on as usual, in its usual mad way. Rick was thrilled with our baby, and the partying didn't stop and I didn't want it to. We were both happy and enjoying life. The band weren't doing any live work after the tour. Rick hates not working because he goes into a kind of lull and can't get out of it. Of course, he moans when he's on tour: 'I can't wait for this tour to end.' But he doesn't mean it. After two weeks at home he starts going stir crazy.

Francis is completely different. Francis loves to be at home looking after his Koi carp. He's got loads of them, I think they've all got names and they're not your average fish. He pays thousands for them and loves watching them. Rick and I always thought it would be like watching eggs boil — bloody boring! But Francis loves his fish and they have a very long life.

Rick was content. The album did quite well and there were plenty of TV interviews and personal appearances and,

Patty Parfitt

in what little spare time there was, we were redecorating the flat.

We had a lot of good mates. We never — or very rarely — socialised with the band, even Francis and Andy, but we saw the Tarrants, Chris and Ingrid, who are great fun and were very good friends. Ingrid and I became close and Chris is a great laugh, although when he drinks he tends to get suddenly pissed and then falls asleep — I'm not surprised the hours he works. When we were at the Mayfair hotel for my 40th birthday, he went off to the gents. Half an hour passed without him reappearing so we sent Rick in to see if he was OK. Rick found him perched on a loo seat fast asleep! He emerged sleepily only to repeat the whole performance an hour later, at which point Ingrid took him home!

Rick and I both missed Ron, his driver, and Ron's wife Claire. The four of us had enjoyed some fantastic, mad weekends and we were all very close. We used to chill out by choosing a hotel for a weekend — always a good one — then booking two suites and going there to party, party, party. We — at least me, Rick and Ron (Claire was much better than the rest of us) — used to drink too much and do too much coke. It was wonderful fun and we laughed until our sides ached.

Once, we were all so out of it that Ron even lined up on a coffee table in the foyer of an ultra-posh seaside hotel. No one took a blind bit of notice — even the waiter who brought our drinks and had to balance the tray on the edge of the table so as not to disturb the lines of coke.

Rick was still doing quite a lot of coke and I used to join him, although for every four or five lines of his I'd do one. I soon realised I couldn't cope — it did my head in. I'd get terrible headaches. Also, it gives me verbal diarrhoea which used to embarrass me sometimes. I'd have one line and I could hear myself jabbering away nineteen to the dozen — I still do but at least I'm in control. But it was the hangovers in the morning that really persuaded me to cut down. We'd be drinking as well — usually champagne and wine — which is not a good mixture and the hangovers were hell. Another thing was that coke often burned my nose. You obviously can get different grades of it and some of the stuff we used to take was cut with Ajax or something horrid.

But once I was pregnant with Harry I stopped all that. It wasn't worth it.

The band, with the new line-up of Rick, Francis and Andrew, plus Jeff Rich on drums and John 'Rhino' Edwards on bass, were doing well and, more importantly, the money was starting to come in so we could actually pay some bills. Rick hadn't changed — he was still hopelesss with money.

A big cheque would come in and Rick would go: 'Great, I'll go and spend that!'

And I'd try to grab it, shouting: 'No! We need that to pay some bills!'

'Oh, sod that,' says Rick and off he'd go and before you could say 'overdraft' there would be another new car outside the house!

He did make efforts. We set up a company called RPUK which was supposed to be Rick and Patty UK. But when the typist typed it all up she typed it as Rick Parfitt UK. Rick was annoyed but I couldn't care less. So I said: 'Leave it. It's silly — what difference does it make? And anyway all the documents would have to be typed up again.'

I had half shares in the company and was a director which Rick wanted, he said, to prove his love. However I never forgot whose money it was, and I never abused that. Rick used to ask why I didn't buy things for myself, why I just bought things for the house, Harry or him. Rick would buy me anything I wanted anyway, and I was happy with that.

Patty Parfitt

The company made financial sense. When the band does a tour all the money goes into the band's company, which was called Acklode. Money from recordings would go into another company. Then the companies would pay each member of the band their respective take. In our case the monies would be paid into our own personal company and only Rick and I were signatories. At least it was just Rick and I to start with. Later on, when we were splitting up, Rick added a third and fourth signature — the manager David Walker and Alex the accountant — to stop me taking more than I needed. Me!

But early on it was just me and Rick.

The band were about to record a new album and they decided to record it in Nassau in the Bahamas. I was four months pregnant by then, and Rick and I hadn't even had a honeymoon so we thought we'd go out in advance and have some time to ourselves. Just me and Rick and the bump with all that lovely scenery. How romantic!

Rick and I had had some fantastic trips with the band since I'd got back from Australia. We'd been all over the place: Austria, Switzerland, Germany, France, Ireland. I can't remember them all, but the best trip of all was to Sun City, the independent gambling state in South Africa.

It was a controversial trip because the country was still governed under apartheid. But Sun City wasn't. Even so, most artists refused to go there.

Quo said that they would never play before segregated audiences, but the audiences were mixed in Sun City so what was the problem? And, typically, the more people criticised them, the more they were determined to go.

The music industry even banned them from playing live in Britain for three months on their return.

When we got there we were amazed to see photos on the walls of other stars who had come before. Many of them were such hypocrites. Some admitted they'd played Sun City

Laughing All Over The World

— others kept very quiet about it. We looked at the photos; there was Cliff, Shirley Bassey, the Moodies, Queen and Tom Jones. Frank Sinatra had played the first show, and there were many more.

We all stayed in Johannesburg for a couple of nights and then travelled to Sun City, which was one of the most amazing places I've ever seen.

All around is African bush, parched and bare, and then suddenly there's this oasis with fountains, extraordinary luxury hotels, with flamingos walking elegantly across the perfectly mown lawn surrounding the lakes. It was beautiful, and everywhere there were cool ponds, many of them filled with Koi carp — Francis was, of course, in heaven.

The hotel was about a ten star and a good time was had by all. The gig went well. People said that only rich blacks could afford to go to gigs in Sun City, but I studied the audience carefully and have to say I disagree.

Sun City is awash with casinos, and we all had a go and a good laugh. When I won the jackpot — about £200 — on one fruit machine, and the coins came tumbling out and onto the floor, it was the icing on the cake and Rick and I were in stitches.

Almost as soon as we arrived Crux announced that he and his wife Jo were going off on a safari alone. That pissed the band off somewhat, but it couldn't spoil what was a magic time. They reappeared for one or two shows but then they disappeared into the bush again!

Rick and I had visions of the Bahamas being similar — perhaps not as grand, but certainly a little piece of paradise.

We arrived in Nassau, and the first thing that happened was that the flight was late and the bags weren't on it — except one of Rick's. Never mind, we were on our way to this beach house which sounded fab. A guy from the studio picked us up and we snuggled up in his pick-up truck, Rick's hand on my bump, and made our way to the house

Patty Parfitt

— which was on the beach but run-down, hideous and goddamn awful.

Rick was beginning to get in a mood. He wasn't having any of it and I didn't blame him.

The band were due to be staying at the studio in some 'pretty' little cottages that surrounded it. So the guy took us there instead.

Rick took one look. The studio was old, run-down and decrepit. Quo were due to be the last band who played there before it was demolished — or bought up and refurbished!

Rick took a look.

'Oh God, no. I don't like this.' He turned to the studio guy: 'Take us back to the bloody hut.'

It was hardly the Ritz — a shanty thing, terrible. Obviously it hadn't been decorated for years, there was a gas stove with two little rings in the corner, an old stone sink and a couple of cupboards and peeling walls.

'No,' said Rick. 'Take us to the Sheraton Hotel.'

I heaved a sigh of relief.

At the Sheraton there was no room service, and Rick had to get really stroppy to force them into getting us a cup of tea. 'It's 11 o'clock at night, we've just had this hideous journey on the banana boat, my wife is pregnant and we want a cup of tea!'

Tea duly arrived — two plastic cups, a sad looking tea-bag in each and powdered milk – lovely!

'Could we have some towels?'

'Towels? Um ...'

Then Rick had to drive backwards and forwards looking for the luggage. Hopefully it would come in on the 3.00am flight — and hopefully the hillbilly truck the studio guy was driving would get him to the airport and back safely.

He finally arrived back at 4.00am, sweltering by now in his leather trousers. I was curled up in bed. I think the final

Perennial stars – Rick and Francis playing a gig at the Brixton Academy 1996.

Fatherhood – Rick was absolutely thrilled with Harry. We'd just come home from the hospital in June 1989.

Top: Rick and Ron Brown, close friend and driver, on Rick's boat Silversun, summer 1989.
Bottom: Rick Parfitt the rock star at home in the sitting room at Silverdale.

Rick rocks on – live at Wembley, one of Quo's regular venues.

Top: 'Working' on *Perfect Remedy* in Nassau!

Bottom: Quo and entourage backstage at Reading Festival, 1986. This was the first festival minus Alan Lancaster.

Top: Rick, Bernadette and Pip, Quo's producer. Bernadette was to become Rick's first foray into infidelity.

Bottom: The Parfitt family at Christmas 1991, smiling bravely for the camera. This was to be the last Christmas we spent together, and I was desperately unhappy.

Top: Rick and Harry enjoying the pool at Silverdale that so nearly could have killed Harry.

Bottom left: Rick performs his famous out of his head sliding down the wall trick in happier times.

Bottom right: My birthday in Jersey. Rick had just told me that he had been on holiday to Lanzarote with ex-wife Marietta. I very nearly took advantage of the cliff behind me.

Top: By now we had split up, but Rick showed up to take Harry to school for his first day.

Bottom: The winning team! Sports day at Harry's primary school – he won a first prize and I won the Mum's race!

Laughing All Over The World

straw was that there was no key to the mini-bar. There was definitely some booze in there, as Rick found when he rattled the fridge — but no key. Torture!

The honeymoon was not getting off to a propitious start, and I thought it was a good idea if Rick had a drink as soon as possible. The next day, Christmas Eve, the sun shone and we decided to go back to the beach hut.

'We'll go to the supermarket and get some food,' said Rick. 'The sun is shining. The hut will probably look better in the daylight.'

'It doesn't, Rick,' I said with a smile when we arrived. 'But let's make the best of it.'

They didn't sell turkey, so we bought a couple of chickens and some veg. We didn't have a fridge so we found a cool box. The chicken wouldn't fit in the oven, so Rick chopped its legs off and even then it took four hours to cook and was half raw inside. I managed to do some gravy, and we sat there watching the telly as you do on Christmas Day, except the satellite dish to America had broken. All we could get was Bahamian TV, which is seriously religious and consisted of a succession of preachers!

It should have been hell. But it wasn't. I look back on those days fondly. Tired and grubby after the flight, it had all been a bit much but once we'd relaxed we couldn't stop laughing. The whole thing was hilarious. And they say a rock star's life is glamorous.

We finally moved into one of the 'pretty' cottages by the studio, and managed to hire a car — 15 years old — from the Sheraton. We collected the rest of the band from the airport when they arrived after Christmas. The producer was there and so was everyone else — except Francis. He had broken up with Paige by this time, and was with Eileen who was eight months pregnant, so he was coming on later.

We were feeling quite jolly by then, so they all piled into the car and truck, and we took them off to our 'villa'. I

Patty Parfitt

made loads of cocktails, which we drank on the beach while they hung around waiting for their own 'pretty villas' to be prepared. Then we took them to the said rooms, and there was silence and then ... a collective 'Oh'.

Rick and I were in in hysterics.

Jeff the drummer, his wife Helen and two kids arrived next. Then the studio people, and finally Francis and Andrew. So there we all were, one big happy family! The wives, girlfriends and kids were hustled off to lie on the beach while the band got on with some work which turned out to be something of a joke.

It hadn't taken Rick long to suss out the nearest coke dealer, who unfortunately lived just down the road. Coke is big business in Nassau and apparently a lot of it makes its way there before being smuggled on to the mainland USA uncut.

I suddenly thought: 'So this is why we've come here!' You didn't buy it by the gramme in Nassau, you bought it by the bucket! The bowls were honestly huge — and the band's eyes lit up like street lamps!

Rick, the producer and Ian Jones went to do the deal and I don't think they enjoyed the experience. You don't muck around with these guys, who are all there with their minders carrying guns. But the deal was successfully done.

But as for the album — no one did much work after that.

A hell of a lot of coke was done and a lot of drinking, too, although, of course, I couldn't touch either. We all spent New Year's Eve together partying around the pool at the studio. Even Francis joined in. Well, he had no choice really, there was nowhere else to go. What's more he enjoyed it — although he'd hate to admit it! It was great fun although the coke got a little out of hand sometimes. It was funny watching everyone getting out of it when I was sober.

Probably because there was so much coke about, Rick indulged in one of his other pleasures — dressing up in women's clothes. He wore my knickers at home sometimes and occasionally he liked to wear my dresses. I don't know if it turned him on — it certainly didn't do anything for me. But sometimes he'd wear one of my dresses at home. He didn't want to make love in a dress, he just liked to walk around in one in the privacy of our home.

In Nassau he didn't give a damn who saw him. He used to wear one of my pregnancy dresses and a little top. He just got bored.

Men are always in trousers and restricted — he used to like to swing about underneath, like a man wearing a kilt.

Sometimes he liked to wear lipstick as well but only when he was out of it, and it really didn't bother me. It was harmless.

In Nassau, after all that coke he took to walking around in my clothes day and evening. Then the producer thought this looked like fun and he started dressing the same. It was most weird.

Rick loves make-up, too. He's OK about putting on lipstick, but he couldn't cope with mascara, he couldn't handle the brush. So sometimes I'd do his make-up for him and he liked that. Rick always loves it when he's made up for television or some kind of show, some of them sit there grimacing but Rick genuinely enjoys it.

'Why?' I asked.

'Because it gives me a look of perfection,' he said.

'No, it doesn't,' I said. 'It hides your face.'

The band had obviously seen it a few times before. So while Rick was sashaying around the pool, all you'd get from the rest of the lads was: 'Oh, that's nice Rick. Not your colour though.'

We spent two happy weeks in Nassau. After that all I could think of was the birth of our baby.

Like most first-time mums I was looking forward to it, but nervous at the same time. The baby was due on June 10th and as the time got nearer I got huge. Rick was wonderful, loving and attentive and he seemed almost as nervous as

Patty Parfitt

me. He treated me with kid gloves and when we were in the car he'd drive really slowly, carefully avoiding all the potholes — not Rick at all!

The date came and went and a week later I was still at home, bigger than ever. Our doctor lived downstairs so I went to see her.

'Never mind avoiding the potholes,' she said. 'You get Rick to take you out, have a drink, eat a curry and tell him to drive over every pothole he can find on the way home.' So that was what we did. It didn't work. The following morning I woke up feeling sick, with a stomach upset — and no baby.

I thought: 'I'll kill that doctor.'

On June 19th, Rick drove me to Queen Charlotte's hospital in Hammersmith where they were going to induce me. It was quite late at night so he saw me in and then went home. The hospital called him at 5.00am and told him to come quickly because labour had started.

He arrived in a flash — God only knows how fast he drove — and the police actually stopped him for speeding. But when he told them where he was going they let him off — and gave him a police escort! Once there, Rick was great, fooling around as usual. We'd booked an epidural but I really wanted to try and do without, so they gave me gas and air which Rick commandeered as soon as he arrived.

'Mmmm,' he said. 'I like this.'

But all my good intentions went out of the window as the contractions grew stronger.

'Fuck this,' I screamed. 'Get me an epidural!' Rick beat a hasty retreat, as he has a real needle phobia. The very thought of a needle makes him feel sick. So he went out and had a fag.

With the epidural I was fine, although I felt stoned out of my head and I couldn't stop talking. No change then! I hadn't a clue what was going on. Rick was down the other end looking, and I vaguely remember him going a bit pale but I just carried on rabbiting on to one of the nurses who was standing by my head.

Then Rick moved around so I couldn't see the machines which were monitoring me and the baby. I've always had a heart problem, diagnosed when I was 20, but I didn't even think of that at the time.

Suddenly three more doctors appeared from nowhere. There I was with with my legs wide open, and they're all looking at me and all I could think of was: 'Great, bring everyone in, have a party, why don't we?' I was embarrassed but still talking away.

What I didn't realise was that the umbilical cord was round the baby's neck. The baby was in distress, and apparently so was I, my dodgy ticker was playing up.

'You could lose your wife or baby,' they told Rick. Poor Rick. I was OK, I was stoned. I didn't know all this until two days later.

Then, as Rick puts it, they got out the shears. He was looking and I heard him say: 'Fuck!'

He looked at me, and held my hand tight: 'You all right? You all right? You sure you're all right?' Sweat was pouring off his brow and he kept grabbing my gas and air.

And then suddenly there he was — Harrison John Parfitt, whom we call Harry. Born at 11.18am on 20 June 1989. Weighed in at 7lb 11oz and he was perfect, just perfect. They wrapped him in a towel and were going to give him to me.

'No,' I said. 'Give him to his Daddy first.' I think looking at Rick holding our newborn Harry was the happiest moment of my life. Rick was all teared up and said to me: 'I've always loved you, I always will.'

I stayed in hospital for a few days, because they wanted to keep an eye on me, and on Harry because he'd had a traumatic birth. But Rick was with us most of the time

Patty Parfitt

although he had to keep popping to the studio down the road to do some work. I was full of stitches and when I got home they hurt like hell which took off some of the gloss off motherhood.

And then it was time for Rick to go into hospital — for his face lift. Or, as I call it, his face drop.

Many people might think that three weeks after the birth of your baby when your wife is still stitched up, in agony and exhausted isn't really the ideal time to go into hospital for a face lift. But I was used to Rick's incurable impatience by now!

One of Rick's favourite expressions, repeated often, is 'I had more chins than a Chinese phone directory!' He was anxious to get rid of some of those chins — not all of them because he didn't want to look as if his skin had been stretched, as some people with facelifts do.

He was also desperate to keep it a secret — he was terrified the Press would get wind of it. I don't think even the band knew about it for ages. He booked into the Harley Street Clinic in London under the surname Beeden — my maiden name — and off he went leaving Harry and me at home.

We picked him up in the car two days later — me and Harry, he wanted me to bring the baby because he'd missed him. We drove home carefully. We couldn't do anything else because my stitches were still killing me.

Once home Rick just crashed out. He was still very woozy and he had stitches and staples along his ear, right around the back of his head to his other ear and up his forehead. He also had a stitch on his cheek where they'd removed a mole.

I had to bathe the stitches in salt water and a special solution four times a day and it didn't take me long to see that they'd made a complete mess of it.

I've seen plenty of stitches before and usually the skin is flat and tight and the stitches are neat and tidy. This skin was kind of gathered, overlapping, pleated like curtains and the stitches were all over the place.

Despite the bathing they also quickly developed a slight infection.

Rick was feeling very sorry for himself and I didn't blame him.

'What does it look like, it looks all right, doesn't it?'

'Yes, fine,' I told him. Well, I could hardly say it looked a fucking mess.

He couldn't eat solids, only sloppy things like soup or mashed food. He was in a bit of a state. So was I. We were a right pair — me walking around like John Wayne without the horse and him looking like something out of *The Addams Family*.

Even so, we went to the Isle of Wight two days later. We'd been invited to be on the start boat for one of the big races at Cowes week, and Rick was determined to go. He loves boating and he wasn't going to miss out and I had to go, too.

So he dressed up, wearing his Captain's hat, dark glasses and a scarf wrapped around his neck, which practically obscured his whole face, and off we went. My sister babysat Harry just for the day and I drove. Rick couldn't because he couldn't turn his head.

It was a good day except for Rick not being able to move his head, and my stitches were giving me hell. I drank far more than I should have, which deadened the pain. Then I drove home. I shouldn't have done that — even now I feel a bit ashamed. A stretch of the A3, the Portsmouth Road, still makes me shudder.

Back home Rick crashed out and the following day I went to see our doctor downstairs. I was in such pain. I kept thinking: 'This can't be right.'

'Christ!' she said looking at them. 'They're all infected. You've got to get to the hospital. Why on earth didn't you come to me before?'

Patty Parfitt

So I went back to Queen Charlotte's where they took all the stitches out, and then did them all over again. Ouch!

But Harry more than made up for all the pain. He was such a lovely baby, and he's such a lovely boy now. The dead spit of Rick. As Dayle says: 'The spit in Rick's eye.' A quaint Aussie expression.

Rick went back to his doctor, who said that his stitches were healing well. When Rick told me that I bit my tongue, I had to. Then he had the stitches out, although I still had to keep bathing the scar.

He kept gazing at himself in the mirror.

'What do you think? You can see the difference, can't you?'

'Yes, yes of course,' I kept saying. In fact, I couldn't really see any difference at all. OK, some of the chins had gone and you could see a bit more of his jaw line, but as he'd been losing weight I think that would have happened anyway.

One side of his face was still completely numb. He used to slap himself hard and say: 'Look, I can't feel that at all.'

'Stop it, you'll hurt yourself.'

He asked the doctor about it.

'Quite normal,' he said. 'It will go in three weeks or so.'

That was in 1989. Rick left us in 1993 and he still had no feeling on one side of his face by his ear. I thought he'd been stitched up in all senses of the word. £10,000 for that!

I told him to go back to the hospital. But his response was typical: 'Fuck it. I'm not going back. If it's there, it's there.'

But despite our physical woes life was good. We were both besotted with Harry.

His birth made the papers, and the press came along to take pictures of us. We were proud as anything.

'I didn't expect it to be such a thrill,' Rick said to one of the reporters. 'Although I've had kids before, this was the first time I've been at the birth and it was exhilarating. Until then I don't think I realised quite what women have to go through. You're wonderful, you lot!'

And he went on: 'From the first second I saw him, I knew I would dedicate my life to him. I want to be there to watch him growing up. I wasn't able to do that with my other kids and I'm only now realising what I missed.'

Oh my Ricky. It didn't turn out quite like that, did it?

14

Down the Dustpipe

Rick and I were really looking forward to moving into our new house, Silverdale, in Walton-on-Thames. It was previously owned by Mike Yarwood, the comedian, and it was a fabulous place. It was huge — it had seven bedrooms and numerous bathrooms. Ours was fantastic with a vast, sunken, gold-plated bath, jacuzzi, loos and bidets for both of us, and a sunbed. I loved it and Rick and I often had baths by candlelight. Rick's a real candle freak, he loves being in the bath with no light, just the candles and he got me into that, too. Heaven.

There was an enormous kitchen, dining room and reception hall, several lounges and a vast music room with nice leather chairs and desks. I put a lot of Quo's albums on the wall and Rick had all his guitars in there. He loved that room and it actually made him enthusiastic about writing.

The outdoor heated pool was big and the gardens exquisite. When we were still at Quay West, Rick and I had gone

Patty Parfitt

shopping at the Boat Show to buy a new toy — a £75,000 motor cruiser called *Silver Sun*. Rick's always been crazy about boating. It was moored at Shepperton and we had some wonderful days out on the river. It was bliss.

It was all very different from the flat at Quay West which was really quite small. That had balconies overlooking the river but only two bedrooms, one bathroom and a kitchen area at one end of the lounge.

But in one important way Quay West had the edge over Silverdale. We had been happy at Quay West. Silverdale wasn't a happy house. Mike Yarwood had suffered a nervous breakdown and marriage break-up while he lived there. It wasn't happy for us either.

But to begin with we were thrilled with it, especially Rick who loved posing for pictures in front of it, behind it, in the gardens and on the roof! His expression in those photos says it all: 'Hey! Look at me, I'm the rich rock star!'

Rick had been seeing his son, Richard, on and off, although recently the visits had petered out. Once at Silverdale, we began to see more of him again. We invited Richard to come on the boat with us, and it was great fun. Rick took him home to his mum, Marietta, after the visits, or, if he'd been drinking he'd get him a cab, but usually he drove Richard back himself, and I didn't think anything of it. We were happy. Life was good. It really seemed to me that everything was fine.

Of course, we had the odd argument, as all married couples do. Most of our arguments were about Rick doing too much coke. They started when I got pregnant and then had Harry.

'We've got to clean up our act,' said Rick.

And I'd say: 'We?! Not *we*! *You*!'

That one was in Nassau. But it didn't make much difference — the partying went on. Once Harry was born Rick did calm down, at least for a month or so. Anyway we simply couldn't keep up the pace with a newborn baby, and to both of us

Laughing All Over The World

Harry came first. Also, Harry had to go into hospital when he was only tiny because he wasn't eating properly. He was dehydrating badly.

Rick and I were frantic. Everything Harry ate he threw up, and he had no energy so he had to spend some time in hospital. I stayed with him on an iron bed by his cot.

Rick was wonderful and would stay to give me a few hours break, but it was worrying for both of us. Fortunately Harry was fine, he just had some kind of tummy infection.

A little later, when Harry was toddling, we had a truly terrifying near-miss with him. When Rick was with Marietta, she insisted on having a pool because she liked to work out in water and swimming was the only exercise she did. Rick used to go mad because she insisted on having the pool heated all the time and it cost a fortune. Even so, when we moved into Silverdale, Rick was the one who said it should be heated constantly.

He especially loved it in winter when the water was warm and all around it was icy cold. It was lovely but the cost was diabolical; you could have lit the whole road for a year with the electricity bill we had for a week!

Once again the pool didn't have a fence or a gate and we were both very conscious that we had to have one. A man had come round to give us an estimate and was due to start work the following week. I think it's ridiculous that the law doesn't insist that anyone with an outdoor pool has a childproof fence around it.

In Australia, if you don't put up a fence before you fill your pool with water, they come with a bulldozer and fill the whole thing with sand until you do.

When we moved to the house the first thing Harry did was run to the pool and go: 'Wow!' and he toppled on his little feet.

Rick looked at me and said: 'You see. You see how easy it is.'

'Yes,' I said anxiously. I could see then how children might

213

Patty Parfitt

fall in, and then, as we were waiting for the men to start on the fence, that's exactly what happened.

I remember it so clearly, it's like a picture frozen in my mind, a horror picture. It was almost a re-run of what happened to Heidi. Harry was in the TV lounge watching telly with his Daddy. I was in the kitchen and Rick came in to ask me where I wanted to go that night to eat.

'Where's Harry?' I said.

'He's watching TV. I'll go back to him in a second. What do you want to eat tonight?'

'Chinese,' I said.

'Indian,' he said at the same time and we both laughed.

'Go back to Harry and bring him in here. You did shut those doors, didn't you, the French doors?'

Rick's face fell, he rushed past me making a kind of cry and the next thing I heard was a splash. I got to the kitchen window and I could just see Rick's toes as he dived into the pool. My reaction surprised me.

I think my heart literally stopped. I couldn't breathe. I couldn't move. I just looked out of the window then, very calmly, I went to the cloakroom downstairs where there was a shower and picked up two of our big fluffy white towels and walked out to meet Rick who was carrying Harry out of the pool. Harry was going blue. Rick turned him over on his front and pumped his back. Water just spat out, he coughed and I put a towel over him. Rick knew what he was doing. I don't know what I would have done if Rick hadn't been there — I don't know if I would have done that or not.

Perhaps I would have but at the time I couldn't do anything. I froze. I was frightened to touch Harry, I was frightened I'd kill him. I had no tears, nothing, I was frozen with terror.

Harry then started crying so I knew he was OK and Rick said: 'Pick him up.'

I wrapped Harry in one towel, draped another over Rick and started rocking Harry in my arms. Rick threw the towel off and started hitting the grass. He went berserk. He was just on his knees, hitting the grass and crying at God: 'Why *me*? Why the fuck don't you take me? Why are you taking my children?'

He'd totally lost it. I tried to put my arm around him but he shook me off.

I'd never seen him like it and I thought, 'Christ, I must get Harry out of here.'

Harry was still crying but, gradually, he was calming down and I rushed indoors with him and rang the doctor. Fortunately I knew her well — she used to live below us at Quay West.

I told her what had happened.

'What colour is he?'

'He was blue then he looked white, but now the colour's coming back to his cheeks.'

'How long was he down there?'

'Seconds, just seconds. Rick got him out.'

'It sounds OK but I'll come straight over. Keep him warm.'

I put Harry to bed and he seemed drowsy. He was tired after fighting the water.

Rick came slowly into the bedroom. He looked terrible.

'Sorry,' he said.

I said I had to go to the loo but I didn't want to leave Harry.

'I'll stay with him,' Rick said and knelt by Harry's bed. I went to the loo where I vomited. Still I hadn't cried but then I started to shake. I went back to Harry, pulled up the sofa next to his bed and lay there looking at him and holding him so I could feel he was warm. Finally I fell asleep until June our babysitter arrived.

'Come on,' she said. 'Wake up, you're going to get cramp in your arm.' She was right. It had gone completely numb and, however much I rubbed it, it stayed like that for hours.

Harry woke up.

Patty Parfitt

'Juney, Harry fell in the pool,' he said and then seemed perfectly all right. It wasn't until two days later that I started crying my eyes out and I thanked God for our son's life.

Rick and I were shell-shocked, that's the only way to describe it and, after that, Rick's phobia about swimming pools and water grew worse.

When we moved to Silverdale, Paul, Quo's gofer, moved into our old flat in Quay West. Suddenly Rick started going out with him in the evenings. At least that's what he said. Quo weren't working — at least they weren't on the road. They were still doing bits and pieces in between touring and recording, but there was nothing much going on, which Rick always hates. So he and Paul used to go off to various local pubs.

Then they'd come back late and drunk and I was getting fed up with it. Rick began to say: 'I need a bit of a break this evening, I think I'll go out with Paul.'

'No,' I'd say, 'I'll try and get a babysitter. Let's go out together.'

'No, I'm going out with Paul. You just stay here.'

Of course, I found out later that he'd really been going off to see Marietta and Paul was merely covering for him, just as Ron had done for Rick years before. He's very good at getting other people to lie for him.

The worst thing was that I really thought everything was all right. I really did. Then one night Rick came home and I was sitting in the lounge — in one of the many lounges — watching telly. He looked serious — and only slightly pissed.

'I want to talk to you.'

'Good,' I thought.

'I've been thinking about it, and I think we need a break.'

'What do you mean? A holiday?'

But suddenly I realised that was the last thing Rick had been thinking of. I felt sick and panicky; I knew we'd had a couple of arguments that week but nothing heavy, nothing had warned me of this.

'I just don't want this...' and he opened his arms, encompassing the family home. 'I just want ... I don't know what I want. I think I need to be on my own for a while.'

He'd said it. My blood ran cold.

'What about Harry?' It was the first thing that came into my mind.

'I'll still see him, of course. And I'll still see you — I love you but I want some time on my own.'

'Why? What have I done?'

'Nothing. It's not you. You haven't done anything wrong. It's me. You do everything right, you're fantastic.'

That's what he always said: 'It's not you — it's me.'

He continued: 'I'll never divorce you. I'm never going to leave you, so don't think that. I just want to be on my own, it's as simple as that. I'll be back in a couple of months or so. But at the moment I just want to be on my own.'

I was stunned. I didn't quite know what to think. He'd had a few drinks, but for once he wasn't pissed.

What made things worse was that Francis and Rick were planning to do a tax year out — live abroad for a year for tax reasons. So we'd already been in touch with estate agents in Jersey, who were sending us bumph about various houses. I was due to go out there to sort out kindergartens for Harry and June, our housekeeper and nanny, was going to come with us. She'd already made plans to sell her own house or rent it out.

So I couldn't quite believe what Rick was saying. I thought perhaps he was just in a mood. I took it all with a pinch of salt.

And life went on as normal. But a week later Rick came home one night and said: 'I've changed my mind. You're not going to Jersey. I want to be on my own, just for a while. Frame and I are going to stay in the hotel like we did before,

Patty Parfitt

and you can come out and visit. That's what Eileen is going to do.' Eileen by now was Frame's wife.

There was never any question that Eileen would move over. There were just too many children. Francis was a father of six. Most of them were settled in schools in England, and then there was Frame's house, not to mention his Mum and Auntie in residence.

I was absolutely devastated. This was serious. It was almost like a physical pain. I couldn't understand what had gone wrong. But it wasn't the end of our marriage, and I clung to that straw. I knew Rick didn't want that. He kept insisting that all he needed was space, not a divorce. He also swore that he wasn't seeing anyone else.

Lying bastard. I didn't believe him.

And I had good reason not to, because before we moved to Silverdale, Rick had had an affair with his producer's wife. Pip Williams, the producer, had worked with Quo for 30 years, and Rick had known him all that time. Loyalty isn't one of Rick's strong points.

Rick was best man at Bernadette and Pip's wedding along with David Walker. Tradition has it that the best man shags the bridesmaids. Typical Rick — he ended up bonking the bride!

Bernadette was madly in love with her producer and we often used to go out as a foursome.

But then things between us four friends changed. My Mum, who's always had a weak heart, was rushed into hospital to have open heart surgery. She was taken into Southampton Hospital and, leaving June to look after Harry, I got there as fast as I could. Rick was away rehearsing at Bray. I knew Bernadette was around the band but I didn't think anything of it. She was David's PA and she was a close friend.

Mum's condition worsened and my father, my sister and I were there every day. The doctors said if she didn't have an operation she'd die, but she might not be strong enough to survive it. They operated and it wasn't successful, so they had to operate again. We were all sick with worry and, before the second operation, the doctors told us to go in and see her. Basically, they were saying we should go and say goodbye because we might not see her again.

I phoned Rick and begged him to come down — after all, he'd known my mum since we were kids. I needed him. But he said he couldn't, they were in the studio rehearsing and recording and besides the weather was bad. That was ridiculous. I was driving to Southampton in the sleet, snow and driving rain. I didn't care. If your mother's dying you'd drive in a hurricane.

We all kept vigil at the hospital while Mum had another operation, and against all the odds she pulled through, thank you God. Rick finally arrived two days later. Mum was still doped up to the eyeballs, she felt no pain, and she was on a real high, all artificial but it was such a relief to see her alive we didn't care.

'Oh, Mum,' said Rick. 'Whatever you're having, I'll have some of that. It looks great!' She's never forgotten him saying that. When Rick had his operation recently she said: 'The reason he says he's jumping out of bed, feeling fine and playing with the nurses is because they've given him that stuff I was on. I'm not being silly, Patty — I know what it was like. It was great!'

So Rick was sitting on her bed and telling her how much he wanted her to pull through, and how he had desperately wanted to get down to see her but he couldn't. And I just sat on the bed thinking: 'You fucking liar.' I knew something was going on but I wasn't sure what. He went down a lot in my estimation then. I wondered perhaps if he'd been doing a lot of coke so he didn't want to drive. But Quo had their own fleet of cars and drivers so someone could have driven him up.

Now that Mum was out of danger, I felt I could enjoy my

Patty Parfitt

fortieth birthday party and we planned for a group of us to go out to dinner at Langans, the restaurant in Piccadilly.

My actual birthday was a couple of days later and Chris Tarrant played a birthday record for me on his morning show. We laughed as we listened to it: 'Good morning Mrs P, you are 40 today, ooops she told me not to say that!' That night Rick and I went out just the two of us for an Indian meal in Teddington.

I was in a good mood, and we were having a good time until the end of the meal.

'You've heard the talk about Bernadette and Ian Jones having an affair?' I said. There had been loads of gossip flying around about Ian and Bernadette. I said: 'Oh well, he's always around and she's always around so there's bound to be gossip. But I don't believe it. She loves her Pip too much. But what if it is — poor Pip, he's such a nice guy.'

Rick suddenly turned on me.

'Shut up, shut up about poor fucking Pip and Bernadette.'

'What?'

'It was me.'

'What was you?'

'It was me that had the affair.'

I burst out laughing. I was creased up.

'Oh that's good Rick! What, you and Bernadette?'

I couldn't believe it. He'd always said how ugly she was, although she had great legs. Pip wasn't the best-looking bloke in the world but he was good fun. Rick was always telling me how he could never fancy Bernadette, because she was a good friend. 'But those outfits she wears and her teeth go like this when she talks — awful!' And here he was telling me he'd had an affair with her. It was laughable. I just couldn't believe it. She was supposedly a good friend too.

'Shut up,' he said. 'Just shut up! Stop laughing. I mean it. I've been trying to tell you. It's been driving me mad, that's why we've been arguing over the last couple of months.'

Suddenly I realised he wasn't joking.

'When did this happen?'

'Just before Christmas.'

'Just before Christmas? But we all went out to dinner just before Christmas. You, me, Pip and Bernadette.' My God, we'd even spent New Year's Eve together.

'Yeah. It was just the lead up to Wembley.'

Wembley is always the last gig of Quo's tour and it's always just before Christmas. In November the band usually play Ireland.

Rick said: 'That was the one that really hurt me …'

'Oh, it's happened a few times then?' And suddenly I felt an overwhelming, chilling sense of impending doom. Everything was slipping away.

'It went on for a few weeks, well, a few months, I'm sorry. I couldn't get down to see your Mum because I was so out of it. Bernadette was coming down with some coke and I stayed with her for two days.'

I'd been keeping vigil at my Mum's sickbed and he'd been coked up, in bed with Bernadette. I went mad. I was incandescent with rage.

I grabbed my car keys, slapped Rick around the face and stormed out, leaving him in the restaurant.

I drove off in the Range Rover, and then I saw Rick standing in the road. I couldn't drive over him so I stopped, he got in and we went back to the flat. June was there looking after Harry, so we were very polite and got her a car home. But as soon as she'd gone I went mad. I couldn't scream in the restaurant, I could only slap but at home I could scream. It was like a physical pain. I felt so hurt and so betrayed. I just screamed: ' Why? Rick, why did you do this to me?'

'I don't know, I don't know.' He was crying by now.

Just two weeks before, I'd been on a girls night out with

Patty Parfitt

Kim and Bernadette. Rick had said: 'Go on, go out, you don't get out that much now we've got Harry.' And I'd said: 'You don't let me. ' So I'd gone out with the girls — my supposed friends — to The Old Rangoon, a lovely pub in Barnes and we'd had a fab night. It had been a great laugh. No artificial highs — except for a few drinks — we only did coke when we were with the boys.

Both Bernadette and Kim knew! Bernadette was saying what a hard time she was having with Pip, they'd been arguing and there I was, cuddling her and saying: 'Oh don't worry, he loves you, Rick and I understand.' What a stupid cow I was. How humiliating. Rick had made me look such a fool.

I turned on him.

'Why? Why?' I yelled at him again.

He couldn't give me a proper answer.

'You and I have been arguing because we've been getting too close.'

'What's that supposed to mean? You're making me out to be the guilty one, while all the time you've been having an affair with your best friend's wife. And you could have been there saying goodbye to my Mum. You know, you couldn't be bothered to stop snorting and fucking Bernadette when my Mum was dying — your fun's more important! I hope you feel terrible, I hope it fucking hurts, I hope you suffer nightmares over this. You disgust me!'

Rick took it all. Perhaps he thought, like most men do, that confessing would make him feel less guilty but he looked shattered. Good.

Then the coke and drinks came out.

'Calm down, calm down. For Christ's sake have a drink and calm down.'

I had a drink.

'I don't know why I did it. I love you, you do everything for me. I couldn't ask for anyone better and now I've done this.'

Laughing All Over The World

I don't know how Rick manages it: I ended up feeling sorry for him. I must have been mad but I forgave him that night.

The following day I rang and put David and Kim out of their misery.

'Thank you for being a great friend to Rick and thanks for being bastards to me!'

'But we did it for you Patty,' they said.

'Oh, don't.'

'So you wouldn't be hurt.'

'Fucking look at me now! Why didn't you stop it, why didn't you tell him, why did you let it go on for all that time?'

'I'm not holding his flaming hand, Patty,' said manager David Walker. Oh no?

So that was that. Bernadette and Pip split up for a while but they got back together, just like me and Rick. I made a big pile of all the presents that Bernadette had bought us over the years: the vases, the statues, baby things for Harry. I put them all in a black bin liner and took them around to Bernadette's. She was out but her Mum, who's a lovely Irish lady, was there.

I said: 'I've got all these things that Bernadette gave us. You've obviously heard.'

Bernadette's Mum looked nervous — and sympathetic.

'I'm so sorry for you and the baby.'

'I can't believe your daughter would stoop so low. I hope it disgusts you as much as it disgusts me. I'm glad she's not here. I tell you what, if she was, I'd slap her — no, I'd punch her fucking lights out!'

Bernadette's mum nodded sagely but she didn't say much. Well, what could she say? Then I dumped everything in the bin bags in their lounge.

'Leave it and let Bernadette sort it out. She'll know it's from me.'

It wasn't a very cool thing to do but it made me feel a hell of a lot better.

Patty Parfitt

But Pip was loyal to her.

'We're OK now,' he told me. 'How are things with you and Rick?'

'Fucking awful,' I said. And they were. I loved Rick, and now we had our beautiful baby boy. But I lost it. I didn't lose the love but I lost respect for him. For six months after that terrible episode we were at each others throats.

Bernadette and Pip split up again, and within months she'd moved in with a guitarist from some band or other. What happened to her after that I have no idea.

But Rick and I slowly got it back together and that's why moving to Silverdale was important for us.

'New start,' he said. 'Let's move, let's get a great house. Let's start again. We belong together.' I agree. I've always felt that.

So even when he said he didn't want us to go with him to Jersey, even when he said he wanted time on his own, I couldn't believe it was the end.

Christmas was coming up, and since we were living in this fabulous house Rick and I decided to push the boat out, have all the family around and make it a Christmas to remember.

It was — it was the last Christmas we were together. It was the goodbye Christmas — although I didn't realise that at the time.

We had seven bedrooms in that house but although Rick wanted the family Christmas, he didn't want everyone to stay. My sister and brother-in-law came down, my Mum and Dad from Swindon, Rick's Mum and Dad, the aunties, the nieces and the cousins. It was a good time, just what a Christmas should be, but underneath I was hurting like hell. Rick's tax year started on January 2nd or 3rd and then he was going to leave me. But I couldn't tell a soul. I didn't for months. I kept all the hurt inside me, all to myself.

Meanwhile we wore the Father Christmas hats, pulled the

Laughing All Over The World

crackers, we drank, laughed and ate. Rick and I put on a very good show and, young as he was, Harry loved it all.

Come the New Year, Rick left and he never came back to Silverdale again. Harry and I stayed on and then after three months we moved again to another house in Burwood Park. It was lovely, but smaller.

I still hoped it would all come right. I still couldn't believe we would split up. We belonged together. We always had. But then it started to get messy.

Rick rang me and said that the band were having a week off from touring, and he wanted to go to Lanzarote. He was in Spain at the time so it made sense.

'I just want to go there for a week to chill out. The band's not working, I don't want to go back to Jersey so I'm going to get some sun on my own.

'But if I get really pissed off after a couple of days will you come out? I'll ring you when I get there and let you know the number.'

Of course I said yes. I thought: 'Just let him have his space.' Space. I hate that word. I think 'space' is the word men use when they're lying.

He came back and worked with the band, and then he rang me and said he was going to go back to Lanzarote again. I found out later he went with Marietta. By this time she'd moved back to Germany because she couldn't get a job over here; she had no qualifications. Rick, I knew, had lent her £30,000.

'Do you mind?' he'd said. 'It's for Richard mainly.'

'No, of course not. He's your son.'

'She'll pay it back.'

'Fine.'

Sometimes I look back and can't believe how naïve and stupid I was. After all that had happened, even then I didn't twig. Besides Rick was still coming over to England

Patty Parfitt

occasionally and we'd have a mad weekend together. One weekend June looked after Harry while we went to a hotel in Shepperton and got completely smashed. The room got smashed too as Rick was so drunk he kept falling on things like coffee tables and potted plants and breaking them. And if anything like a chair got in his way while he was stumbling around the room he'd throw it out of the way.

The following day Rick had an important studio job to do and Barry, his driver, came to pick him up leaving me, a wretched but happy and hungover woman still in bed at 4.00pm in the afternoon.

When Rick left in the car he took my credit card with him, and the hotel wouldn't let me leave until I'd paid the bill and paid for the damage. So I rang Rick at the studio and said: 'You've got my gold card.'

'Oh shit. Get June to come around with some money to pay for everything.' Then there was a pause.

'I'd better go,' I said.

'Um, I've just told the band that we're splitting up.'

I couldn't believe it — not after the sexy night we'd just spent together.

'What do you mean we're splitting up?'

'You know, what we talked about, that I'm going to have some time on my own.'

'Well, that's not splitting up is it? Or is there something you didn't tell me last night?'

He sounded sheepish. 'Oh, I put that all wrong didn't I? Come out to Jersey for your birthday — it's only a couple of weeks away.'

OK. I never could say no to the bastard.

Another nasty thing happened while Rick was away. Paul the minder had been away with him at the time — and it was the ideal opportunity for me to go to the Quay West flat to get some things left there when we moved to Silverdale.

I wanted to get the rest of the papers out of the chest of drawers downstairs. I didn't like keeping our papers there but I just hadn't got around to picking them up.

But when I opened the drawer I was in for a shock. There were airline tickets to Lanzarote — via Amsterdam. Not just for R. Parfitt but for M. Parfitt too. Marietta. I couldn't believe it! I was quite honestly dumb-struck. Marietta! It couldn't be.

I confronted Rick about them when he stayed with us two nights later. I worked myself up into a right state and I threw them at him.

'What have you got there?' he said.

'I was clearing out the drawers at Quay West, wasn't I? And I found these. Where you put them.'

'What the fuck are they?'

'You know what they are Rick! They're airline tickets. Lanzarote. M. Parfitt. That's not me Rick, I didn't go. It wasn't me or Richard.'

He said: 'Who the fuck has made these up? I can't believe you are giving me them.' He reckoned that someone was playing a dirty trick on us and had forged the tickets. He screamed at me, got hold of me and shook me. He said: 'You honestly believe I would do that? Walk into an airport with Marietta, go off on fucking holiday, you believe that? How dare you. I thought better of you, Patty.'

He started screaming and throwing things about. He said: 'I just can't believe it. When I find the fucking bastard who has done this to me, they're dead, bloody dead! I don't care if I swing. How dare they do that to you!'

Rick was livid. At least I thought he was. I actually believed him — probably because I really wanted to.

I said: 'Someone has done it, but why would they do this?'

'I don't fucking know, but if I find out it's a fucking friend of hers and they're trying to wind you up ... Oh Patty, I can't believe you thought that of me.'

Patty Parfitt

He stormed out of the house and I ran down the road after him.

'Ricky, Ricky, come back. I'm so sorry. Please forgive me, please forgive me.'

'All right, all right, darling. How could you think I'd do that to you? Oh, Patty, please come to Jersey.'

In fact he met me in Guernsey — at the airport. In a long black, stretch limo, armed with champagne and a big bunch of flowers.

We had a wonderful night at a hotel we'd been to many times — no coke, just drink and not too much of that either so we woke up feeling like humans for a change. The next day we had to go to Jersey. The hopper plane costs £30 but we would have had to wait a few hours to get one.

Typically, Rick wouldn't have any of that. So at a cost of £2,500 he hired a plane to take us across to Jersey — no wonder he's so often broke. The ten-minute flight to Jersey cost us £250 a minute but at least Rick had fun. He can fly although he hasn't got his pilot's licence, but the pilot let him take the controls so he was like a little boy who'd been allowed a treat. A very expensive treat. It was my birthday but he spent more on himself as usual!

In Jersey we celebrated in style at the hotel where Rick was staying and it was wonderful. Perhaps everything was going to be all right after all. That night, 24 April, we walked along the cliffs. It was freezing but the air was good. We linked arms and felt close. Perhaps it was my own fault that it was all spoiled because I said: 'Those tickets, I'm waiting for you to tell me what happened. You know, who did it? Because you're not going get the chance to kill them — I'll do it myself.'

He held tight to my arm. 'I didn't want to tell you on your birthday — but they are real tickets.'

We stopped walking. I turned and looked at him.

'You couldn't tell me on my birthday?' I was mad as hell. 'You told me on my 40th that you'd had an affair with fucking

Laughing All Over The World

Bernadette, now on my 41st you're telling me you've been on holiday with your ex-wife!'

'We had separate rooms — you can check on that,' he said. We screamed and shouted out there on the cliffs.

He promised me that there was nothing going on, that he just wanted his space for a while. Marietta had written a book about him and Quo and Rick wanted to check it over.

For a while I went crazy. I just couldn't believe it! Marietta! I looked over the cliffs. I wanted to jump.

'This I promise you,' said Rick. 'I fucked up with Bernadette but I'm not going to fuck up a second time. I couldn't do it.' Rick is a great actor. He shouldn't have been a pop star, he should have been an actor because he really is bloody good. And, of course, I fell for it.

I forgave him but I was still deeply hurt. We went back to the hotel. I was crying and he was all over me like a rash, comforting me, talking me round. My heart, if not breaking, was cracking badly, and only a man could say what he said next: 'I know it's a really bad time for me to ask ... but it's the Bruno-Tyson fight. It's a really big fight. Would you mind very much if I watched it?'

'OK,' I said, sniffing back the tears running down my cheeks. At the time I was just numb. Now I look back and laugh. Can you imagine any woman looking at her man as he was sobbing his heart out and saying: 'Sorry — but do you mind if I just watch *Neighbours?*'

Between rounds he gave me cuddles then the bell would go for the next round and he'd be back, glued to the box.

After the fight, we went down to the hotel restaurant for dinner and after that we went to the bar where we met up with a couple who were very friendly. They'd just been away somewhere nice on holiday and I said: 'Sounds lovely.'

'But,' said the wife, 'you and your husband must go to some wonderful places all over the world on your holidays.'

Patty Parfitt

In fact Rick and I have only had two holidays — Nassau and eight days in the Algarve.

'No — my husband doesn't take me ...'

Rick jumped. He was obviously afraid I was going to say '... because he takes his ex-wife!' Suddenly he went beserk and started screaming at me in the bar: 'Don't discuss our fucking private life in front of fucking strangers!' Then he stomped off to our room and, after apologising to the couple who were totally puzzled, I followed.

Rick had no reason to behave like this.

'If you'd fucking well listened to me and let me finish my sentence ... I was going to say that we never went on holiday because you worked so hard and were always travelling with the band ...'

He started shouting at me and I really had had enough. I grabbed his jacket and stormed off. 'I'm going for a walk!'

I did. It was late, it was dark, it was pouring with rain and blowing a gale but I walked along the cliffs. Yes, I did look over and yes, I did think of throwing myself off. Jumping would solve a lot of problems — I wouldn't have to put up with this crap any more. But it was all self-pity and suddenly I saw Harry's face ...

In fact I was lucky not to be blown over the cliffs, the wind was so strong that I had to fall to my knees and crawl away from the cliff edge. I found a bench and sat there in the pouring rain, the raindrops making a salty cocktail with my tears. After a while I could hear Rick calling me in the distance from the darkness but I didn't answer him. I must have sat there for two hours.

Eventually he found me and took me back to the hotel. He'd told the hotel manager that I was missing and the hotel had called the police. The police had arrived in force and were about to mount a search. They called it off. I fell into bed, feeling absolutely exhausted, and slept the deep sleep of the truly wretched.

Laughing All Over The World

We spent the next two days together planning the short time we would now be apart — and the lovely house we would eventually have. We both wanted more children and it was time for Harry to have a brother or sister — and I was 41 years old. It seemed no time at all since I was 18. I couldn't believe how fast the years had gone.

Rick planned to stay on in Jersey to do some writing and then he said he'd be over in a month to see us.

'We'll go out, I'll take you out to dinner. We'll spend some time together with Harry. Don't worry, it will be fine ... I promise.'

We kissed goodbye at the airport. He even asked the customs man if he could go through with me to the departure lounge and the guy agreed. We kissed again, said goodbye again. What I didn't realise was that it really was goodbye. I'm glad I didn't know that then. It would have broken my heart. Instead, that surgery was postponed for a few months.

15

A Mess of the Blues

Divorce is always a messy business, the break-up of any relationship is always unhappy and ours was no exception. Once back in England, Rick rarely rang and every time I phoned him he was out or wouldn't take my calls.

He and Francis decided that they'd finish their tax year in Amsterdam — absolutely fatal for Rick. Apart from all that dope, there was the shopping as well. The shops in Amsterdam are fabulous and when Rick's bored there's nothing he likes better than a good shop. He was still sending me all his statements because I was still organising the money and soon I could see that he was spending thousands on clothes and jewellery. He already had at least eight watches including a Cartier, Phillippe Patric and a Rolex Oyster. The trouble is that when Rick is on tour and waiting in the airport departure lounge he gets fidgety and heads straight for the duty free shop and buys another watch. Cameras are also a favourite. He used to have hundreds of them but when he got divorced from Marietta she was burgled and the thieves nicked them all.

He'd also send me messages with clothes he wanted kept at home: 'Hang on to these and send me out such-and-such with Paul or one of the crew.' It was a ridiculous situation. Sometimes he'd even send back his washing!

Then I noticed that the receipts weren't coming to me — they were being sent to the office. I phoned the bank and said: 'Why haven't I got a statement?' I had my own statement but not the one for Rick's Gold Card.

'Oh, we've been instructed to send it to his office.'

I phoned the Quo office.

'Rick wants the statements sent to him so he can check them.'

'But Rick hasn't the first idea how to check them. He's hopeless.'

Finally I spoke to Rick. He was evasive. 'Um, I just thought it would be easier, you know, to staple all the receipts together and send them to the office.'

'Oh, right.'

It seemed strange but even then I didn't get it. I was still hopeful the marriage would survive. I was still faithful to him and he insisted that he didn't want to break up our family.

'I've decided I'm not going to jeopardise my family again. I did that with Richard and Heidi; look where it got me. I had nothing, I lost the lot. I will never do that again. I wouldn't do it to you, you are my best friend in the world, you are my only friend, the only person who understands me. I know I'm a bastard at times — but you see all that and treat me so well. I could never give you up — and you could never give me up. We are stuck with each other.'

The bit about being his only friend was, at least, true. He was completely off the wall at the time and everyone else was well and truly fed up with him.

Laughing All Over The World

I lived in hope. He phoned me to say that he was coming over to London for just one day. He had to have a meeting with David Walker and he was going to see him for dinner at a hotel near Heathrow. Before that he wanted to go to the studio with him and also to see Harry. He couldn't stay for longer because of the tax thing. He took Harry to the studio, and then came home and played with him for a couple of hours. We couldn't talk because of Harry, but he arranged a limo to go to the airport hotel. We went with him.

At the airport Rick said: 'You've only got to say stay and I'll stay tonight.' I wanted him to but I thought I was being sensible by saying: 'If you stay tonight you'll jeopardise your whole tax year.'

'Just say you want me to and I will.'

'You'd better go, darling.'

He told me later that he was trying to tell me that he didn't want to do what he was about to do. I wish I'd known that then. Instead I thought I was being generous and selfless. I was, in fact, being an idiot.

He didn't meet David Walker at that hotel — he met Marietta. Then he flew back to Amsterdam and she followed later. After that he divided his time between Amsterdam and her flat in Germany. And that, as they say, was that.

Even so, it took a while for it all to sink in. I remember once he rang me from Germany because he'd forgotten his PIN number for his cash card and needed to get some cash out. I could hear this German woman talking in the background so I asked him where he was.

'Er, I'm in a café somewhere in Germany.'

'God, it sounds like that woman's sitting on your bloody lap.'

I found out later that she was.

'It's just a waitress,' said Rick.

In fact, it was Marietta speaking to Richard, her son, in

Patty Parfitt

German. He's fluent, but Rick is hopeless at German so when Marietta doesn't want him to know what she's saying they speak in German. After that I didn't hear from Rick for weeks and weeks. I started to get worried and called management.

'No one knows where he is, Patty,' they lied.

'But he could be lying dead in a gutter somewhere! Find out!'

They were good. They made all the excuses under the sun for Rick. Meanwhile Harry and I moved yet again to Fernwood in Walton. The rent went down again, this time to £3,000 a month.

The penny hadn't dropped. I was under the illusion that we were still a married couple. I didn't know he was back with Marietta and no one informed me. When we moved into the new house I packed all his clothes into the cupboards as usual but somewhere deep inside me I knew I was kidding myself.

Then finally he arrived back in the UK.

Once back in England Rick installed himself at our old flat in Quay West. He was still giving me the old line about spending more time with Richard. He came over and took some of his clothes but it wasn't the reunion I'd been hoping for. Then he sat me down and I knew something terrible was coming.

It was 12 October, 1993, the day after his birthday. Dreadful things always seem to happen to us on or around our birthdays.

He said: 'I want us to sit down and talk. I want to tell you something.

'I was having an affair with Marietta. Well, I am having an affair with Marietta, and she came over to Jersey as well as Lanzarote. We had separate rooms — and then we didn't. That's when the affair really started. But I don't want a divorce, I really don't.'

Laughing All Over The World

'What the fuck do you want?'

'I just want you to let me do my own thing for a few months. May God strike me dead and I know it's appalling but I want to have my cake and eat it, too.'

Funnily enough that's just what his stars said in the *Sun* the following day: 'There is a lot of upheaval in your life because you want your cake and eat it, too.' And mine said: 'You've got to change the manic status quo!'

Rick rambled on while I sat there stunned trying to take in the fact that my husband had left me for his ex-wife. He had left me before I went to Australia in the '70s and married Marietta, then me, now he was with her again — this roundabout was beginning to make me feel very sick.

'I'm going back and mostly I'm in Amsterdam but I sometimes stay with Marietta in her flat. But it's tailing off now. It's just like a buzz to sleep with your ex-wife. I don't love her any more, well, I never did and I told you that before, I love you and Harry. It just went further than I thought it would.'

I couldn't believe what I was hearing.

Marietta! He'd gone back to Marietta! After all the things he'd said about her to me! He used to call her all sorts of names. He hated her for going to the papers slagging him off, he hated her for, as he saw it, turning Richard against him, he hated her for ripping him off for all that money in the divorce — the papers quoted £2 million.

I just couldn't believe he would go back to her. Rick and I had even been trying for another baby before he took his tax year out because neither of us wanted Harry to be an only child.

I listened to him talking and I felt my head about to explode.

'So you'll fuck her up again, will you, and Richard too?' I screamed. 'Richard thinks he's got his Mum and Dad back

239

Patty Parfitt

together, you're really going to fuck him up again.'

'Richard's old enough to understand. He's very happy.'

'Richard is your son and he'll never be old enough to understand. He's been hurt when he was young, he hated you and now he thinks the world of you and then he's going to hate you all over again. You don't know what you are doing to other people! And what about Harry? What do I tell him?'

'You don't tell him anything. You haven't, have you?'

'No. He thinks Daddy's wonderful. I show him videos of you and we sit there and go: "Isn't Daddy clever and wonderful."'

'I'm not going to stay with Marietta, that's going to finish in the next few months. But I'm still not ready to come back as a full-time husband. I think the best thing is that I buy a house for you and Harry, then, when I've finished this tax year, my head will be sorted out. In fact, I think perhaps I'll buy two houses — in the same street — one for you and Harry and one for me. Then I can come to your house or you can come to mine, and when I get my head sorted out we can sell one of them, or both.' He grinned, almost triumphant. 'What about that?'

The man was mad.

Rick looked bewildered at my lack of response. I stared at him, astounded.

'I'm trying to make it clear and easy for you so you won't be hurt.'

I said: 'HURT! This is HURT!' And I whacked him one. 'Fuck right off!' And I belted him again.

'Patty, now don't get upset now ... ouch! ... Patty, now calm down! Ouch! We've got to talk about Harry ...'

'No we don't! FUCK OFF!'

I was pushing him out of the door.

'Don't push me, you don't understand. Ouch! ... I did come to collect some clothes!'

'You want clothes. You can have some clothes, you bastard!'

Then I did something I've secretly always wanted to do. I chucked a load of his clothes out of the top window. The rest I gathered up in my arms and took to the front door where Rick was standing with his mouth open like a goldfish. I threw them at him. And then there were the shoes. I threw them.

'Don't hit the car, it's not mine, it's rented!' he cried, his arms full of clothes as he tried to gather up his belongings from the street, and protect the car at the same time. Rick will always protect his beloved cars.

Well fuck you, Rick Parfitt — Ricky was well and truly dead.

Harry was upstairs. I rushed up and got him dressed and out of the house and into the garage in a record three minutes. The Mercedes was parked right up by the garage door. The garage door was electronic. As soon as I pressed the button it would go up and scratch the Mercedes to bits. Whoopee!

Rick was wandering around picking things up like a blind man. 'Patty, Patty, I didn't mean to upset you!'

Bloody man. I came out of the garage like Batman in his Batmobile — I had a Range Rover and it had bull bars on it.

'Fucking hell,' said Rick. 'The woman's gone mad!'

Unfortunately I missed his Mercedes, albeit by millimetres. Rick tried to be masterful. He put his hand up like an old-fashioned policeman and said: 'Stop that fucking car!'

I leaned out of my window.

'Move your fucking car — or else!'

I think he realised I meant business.

'Oh shit.' He leapt into the Mercedes and started to reverse out of my way and off I stormed — to his Mum's.

I was still shaking when I got there.

'Lil, Rick and I have just split up.'

'What are you talking about, dear?'

Patty Parfitt

I said: 'Surely he's said something to you.'

'No, dear. He said he hadn't seen so much of you but it was going to do you both good.'

'Because he's having an affair with Marietta.'

'Don't be silly.'

'It's been going on for six months, maybe nearly a year. And he's told me about it. That's why I'm here screaming,' I shouted.

'Patty,' said Lil. 'He wouldn't do that, not with her. My Ricky wouldn't do that. Don't be stupid.'

'I'm not stupid, Lil. It's the truth. And he's gone to pick Richard up from school. Then they'll be coming here, and I want you to know that that is *it*! We're finished.'

Lil was upset and didn't know what to say.

'Oh,' she said. 'It can't be true. I don't want him to go back with her, Patty. I don't want to lose you and Harry.'

'You won't lose anyone, Lil. I've finished with your son but I haven't finished with you. I'll see you next week. I'm just going away because I've got to get away from him.'

But that was more or less the last I saw of Lil. Unfortunately Rick's father, Dick died in November 1988. When we split up I left the ashes with Rick; I asked him the other day where they are. He said he has no idea!

When push came to shove, Lil could never admit her Ricky had done wrong. I know how she felt and I've never blamed her for that.

With Harry still in the car, I did what I had often done before when I was upset — drove the A3. It's a straight road and you can go fast. You get to Portsmouth and you can't go any further, and then you just turn round and come back again. I stopped to buy Harry sweets as a treat — he's rarely allowed sweets because I worry about his teeth — and then I very wearily took him home and put him to bed. Then I hit the booze, broke open the wine, any bottles I could find and rang anyone I could think of.

What really annoyed me was that however much I drank, I couldn't get pissed, the adrenalin had taken over making me feel sharp and alert. I rang my Mum and Dad, my sister, I rang Australia, and America, and I wasn't even pissed when I finally got around to ringing Marietta in Germany.

She was cool. 'Can I phone you back Patty, because I've just got in from work.'

I looked at the clock. Good God, it was only 8.00pm. I thought it was really late.

'No you bloody can't,' I said. 'I won't bother you again. I just want you to know I know about you and Rick.'

'I only had an affair with him after he told me he had finished with you,' she said. 'He told me the marriage was over a long time ago. If I'd thought you were still together I wouldn't have gone with him.'

'But I didn't even know it was finished with me! Rick told me it wasn't!'

'Yes, he did.'

'He didn't, Marietta. He told me he was going to see you just until the end of his tax break, and then he wanted to have his and hers houses for him and me in the same street!'

Ironically, I read later in the papers that Rick thought it would be a good idea for him and Marietta to have his and hers houses and gardens.

'Patty,' said Marietta, who was still remarkably cool under the circumstances, but then I suppose she thought she was playing a winner's game. 'Patty,' she said in that irritating guttural voice, 'I would not have hurt a family ...'

'Maybe you wouldn't,' I said. 'But Rick certainly has. He's hurt you and now he's hurt me and Harry, too. Do you know that he's seeing someone else as well?'

Oops, Patty, you bitch — I made that bit up just to get her reaction. Mind you, knowing Rick it was probably true! Later I found out it was — he was seeing Debbie Ash again!

Patty Parfitt

'I don't care,' said Marietta, 'I don't care. He's all I've ever wanted. I'll put up with it.'

'You're stupid,' I said. 'You are so bloody stupid. Don't you realise that you're going to get hurt?'

'But he's changing, Patty. He really is.'

Oh good grief! Stupid woman!

'Too bloody right he's changing. He's changing his colours as it suits him.'

'Can I call you tomorrow, Patty? It is just that I am so tired. I've been at work since six this morning, up since five.'

'Marietta, I really don't give a shit. I've been up for five months.'

'OK. I understand, but can I talk to you another time?'

'No, don't phone me because I will certainly never phone you again. I'm sorry to bother you, Marietta, but I'm hurt and upset. And you will be, too. Goodbye.'

I never did ring her again and, of course, I was right — she was hurt again.

Meanwhile, Rick's Cousin Sue took over looking after Rick and then she became Quo's wardrobe mistress. Their wardrobe mistresses never lasted long because Rick used to come on to most of them and the girls got fed up with it. Most probably wouldn't oblige so Rick would say that they'd have to go. And, at the next gig, another girl would have taken over and the whole business started again.

The band weren't keen on having their families involved in the business. They liked to keep their wives and girlfriends and other family members in a separate pigeon hole.

Francis didn't want Sue working for them but he could hardly complain because he'd just hired his son, Simon, to work as the band's gofer and bagboy.

Sue has always adored Rick. She's known him since he was one day old and if anyone slagged him off she'd always stick up for him and give them a piece of her mind. You didn't mess with Sue — she'd been a store detective.

Then Rick was going to buy a house and he came up with what he thought was a brilliant idea. Sue could leave Ben, her husband and move in with Rick and look after the house. He was quite amazed and annoyed when Sue refused! To Rick it was ideal — he simply couldn't live on his own, he couldn't cope, and he needed her.

But Sue wasn't going to nursemaid Rick. He grew more and more annoyed and the relationship between him and his cousin rapidly went downhill after her refusal.

Sue used to drive Rick because he'd lost his licence and one day he started having a go at her about her driving. It was the last straw for her. She pulled the car over and told Rick: 'I'm not taking this any more.'

'Get out of the car,' he shouted. And she did.

David Walker begged Sue to stay on for just three or four days as wardrobe mistress because the band were playing Wembley. She did — she wouldn't let anyone down.

Rick didn't ring me for a good month after the Batman episode. He was shit scared — he'd never seen me like that before. All of a sudden I wasn't little Patty any more, little Patty who'd put up with anything. I went ape-shit, and I'd pushed him around. I'd never done that before. I could hardly believe it myself that I'd actually hit him. And it wasn't just anger at the affair, it was anger for all the hurt over the years. He bloody deserved it — I only wish I'd hit him harder.

Two days afterwards I read in the papers that Rick celebrated his birthday at the Hippodrome with his sons Richard and Harry. It was all rubbish, of course. Rick was staying away from me — and away from Harry. Harry wasn't with Rick, he was with me.

That Christmas I took Harry to see his Dad play Wembley — I hadn't told him anything. He was far too young. Like most kids he just wanted to know that everything was safe and secure; he had his Mum and Dad even if his Dad was away working most of the time.

June came with us, and she took Harry backstage to meet Rick after the show. I couldn't face seeing him or the rest of the band. I felt a fool, it was all too humiliating. But Andrew's wife Caroline came up to me and put her arms around me and said: 'I'm so sorry, darling. He is a stupid idiot.'

'Well,' I said. 'There you go. What's new?'

Jeff's wife, Helen, came up, too, and told me that she couldn't stand Marietta, which I suppose she thought would cheer me up. 'I met her the other week and she really is a stuck-up snob. Nobody likes her.' Helen was very upset for us.

I felt like saying: 'Well, Rick obviously likes her.' Instead I said: 'Well, I don't really care if they all like her or not, Helen, because I've had enough.'

Maybe a little part of me still thought that Rick was going to come back. After all those years, after all that shared history, after all we'd been through together, I couldn't quite believe that it was all over.

He was the love of my life. But I'd really reached the end of my tether.

There was a record I played again and again at home. It really struck a chord with me. It was by The Beautiful South. It's the one that starts 'I need a little time to think it over ...' That record still hits a chord with me even now.

I was so hurt and I was so angry. Maybe if Rick had played his cards differently I would have had him back even a year after that Batman day. But then I started to get letters about the divorce. He didn't see Harry, and he was hurting Harry, too. I was coping alone with Harry's tears and bed-wetting, tantrums and screaming. I couldn't have borne it.

He tried to come back but he kept Marietta in the background. He would have dumped her if he knew he could move straight back in with me. With Rick, like most men I suppose, he wanted us to overlap. Once he had the next one lined up then he could leave the one he was with. He couldn't risk being on his own. It's like a merry-go-round, a carousel — you get on when you're in favour, you're chucked off when you're not, but you're supposed to sit there on the grass watching it go round and round because who knows when you might be invited to jump on again.

I was fed up with it. I got sick. We had a child. A child was involved. It wasn't a game.

So when Rick called in the lawyers, I got a solicitor too and started contesting the divorce. Fuck it — let battle commence.

But, in my heart, I didn't want a battle. I wanted Ricky. I wanted Ricky home with me and Harry. I didn't want a divorce. I knew Rick didn't want one either. He rang me and told me so: 'I don't want a divorce, I just want to do my own thing. I'll see Marietta but I'll see you. I want to have a bit of fun. Then I'll be back with you and Harry.'

But when I started to object to this plan he started getting angry. I wasn't supposed to object. I was supposed to take whatever crumbs were on offer. In the end he threw the phone down and hung up on me. I just burst into tears.

I don't know how I lived through the months that followed. The pain was physical. But I had to keep going for Harry's sake. Rick even brought Marietta over to England for Valentine's Day and they stayed at the Mayfair Hotel — *our* hotel. It was unbearable.

I didn't hear from Rick — all my dealings were then with the Quo office or between our respective solicitors.

I didn't want a battle, but I was damned if I'd let him walk all over me. I had Harry's future to think of.

So finally we battled it out — by fax and through the newspapers and, at last, we contested it in the courts. But I had no idea that it would all take so long, cost so much, and hurt so deeply. I was drained of all energy.

My weight plummeted to six stone four. I couldn't eat. I hardly slept. I cried at the slightest thing. Sometimes I thought I was going mad.

The months and years crawled by. After we left Silverdale, Harry and I moved five times, the houses always getting smaller and smaller. They were nice houses but it was hard moving all the time. We weren't settled.

It didn't help that I kept picking up newspapers and magazines in which he and Marietta spouted off about how blissfully happy they were to be reunited. It made me actually feel sick. It was all such a load of bullshit.

'I've never been as happy,' Marietta cooed in one article. 'Never. I've never had anything like this in my life. Our love transgresses youth. But there's one condition I make: I will not compete with anyone. If I don't choose to believe that he's faithful there is no point in the relationship.'

Rick then buts in: 'I let Marietta down once but now we've struck up a bond that is even better than before, I won't let her down again. If I did, I'd have to lie and I can't lie to her.' That sounded familiar.

I read on and nearly fell off my chair.

'I have learned that freedom and space are of paramount importance, that romance can go out of a relationship when you live together,' said Rick, presumably with a straight face. 'If Marietta ever came back to live here, she would have her own house and I would have mine, probably within a stone's throw of each other.' Sounded familiar!

Later stories were even more nauseating.

'I used to say, when I was a little girl, that when I grew up I would marry an English gentleman,' said Marietta. 'In the end I married an Englishman who was the antithesis of that ideal. But who knows, ultimately perhaps my childhood vision will come true. Every day Rick becomes more like the English gentleman of my childhood dreams.'

The English gentleman had only recently smashed his latest Porsche on the M3 when he was pissed as a rat and coked up! He was lucky not to have killed anyone — and he was lucky only to have received a small fine and an eighteen month ban. Typically, he blamed me, in the newspapers, for being completely out of it. I hadn't seen him in months.

It was the stress of our marriage break-up which made him do it, he said. He told the magistrates he was deeply depressed because I was using access to Harry as a weapon in our divorce battle. That was rubbish. He'd got the sons mixed up — that was Richard.

I'd never use Harry like that, I'd never keep Harry from his father. It was Rick's choice not to see Harry and Harry got very upset about it. He adores his Dad. But in the three years after Rick left us he only saw Harry twelve times.

In 1994, as the divorce hearing approached, I had spoken for the first time to the newspapers myself, the *News of the World*. I didn't get paid much for the story, and I gave that to Ron to help with his ever-mounting medical costs that his heart problems incurred. I did nothing but tell the truth — that he was paying us just £250 a week while, at the same time, he was spending a fortune on booze, coke and Marietta — he had forgotten how expensive she was! I also said that I still loved him — and I meant it.

Rick retaliated by going to the papers himself. He denied that he'd had affairs when we were married and went on: 'I am not sure that Patty ever really loved me. She has always been obsessed with me, she is just a fan of mine really.'

That hurt — as it was intended to.

Rick and I didn't speak for a long time — we communicated by fax. The faxes flew backwards and forwards.

My faxes went like this one from September, 1995:

Patty Parfitt

'Not content to mess my life up you are succeeding in messing up Harry's, too. You leave it to the last hour to tell him you won't be seeing him because something has come up — you liar, nothing comes up that quick in your business. Harry heard your message and phoned you straight back. I helped him pack his bag, and he was looking forward to going to London but you let him down again. You are so low.'

Rick's faxes usually went like this one from February, 1995:

'11.00am Sunday. Quay West' meaning that was the time and place he'd pick Harry up.

Sometimes he was a little less succinct. Harry left a video at Rick's when he visited him and Rick returned it by dropping it through the letterbox — in a porno video case, *Night Nurse*, which confused Harry considerably.

The next time I saw Rick I gave him back his revolting video case. A fax was soon winging its way to me.

'There was no need to give the porno case to me — *was there* — especially in front of Harry. You could have thrown it away, couldn't you! But no, not you.

'We all know what or who the *filth* is in the house, don't we, Patty, and, by the way, it's not *your* house.

'Harry will tell you what a lovely time we had. There was nothing wrong with him when he left *my house*. You're ill, go and see someone — a doctor or taxidermist maybe. Don't ever send me another fax — EVER.'

My fax back: 'For a start you don't ever tell me what to do. I'll send faxes or whatever I intend to do if I please ...'

And so it went on.

Even poor Harry would fax Rick when he couldn't get hold of him:

'Daddy, why don't you put your machine on? How am I meant to talk to you? I tried your mobile and that's not on. You said I can phone you any time. So why don't you turn it on please.'

The divorce hearing in 1994 lasted for five days. I was with my solicitors and barristers, Rick with his and we didn't speak. Occasionally we'd just look at each other and then look the other way.

I poshed up every day — I wanted to look strong and in control although inside I was hurting like hell and really feeling like shit. I don't know what Rick was feeling, he looked as though he thought the whole thing was just a nuisance.

One day I wore a dress by Moschino — he wore his Thierry Mugler designer suit. The next day I wore a little Chanel suit — he wore his Valentino. Even in this it was a battle, the battle of the designer labels. It was all rather pathetic really. We were granted the divorce nisi but the battle was by no means over. Then the fight about money really started. Rick ran to the papers bleating that I wanted a fortune from him. 'And I just haven't got the money,' he said.

Because of the wrangling about money the divorce wasn't made absolute until 30 October 1996 — two years later. I won the case.

Rick was ordered to pay me £225,000 to buy a house, plus maintenance decreasing over five years, plus £8,000 a year for Harry. He was also instructed to pay the legal bills which came to a staggering £600,000. Rick didn't pay the costs until the end of March 1998 and that's when I got my house money. As I write this I'm still renting. I was glad it was all settled but I wasn't happy. I'd never wanted the divorce. I'd never wanted Rick to leave. Obviously Rick wasn't happy either. They'd got him right in one of the places where he hurts the most — his wallet. The only people who must have been very happy indeed were the lawyers although mine have only just been paid. I don't think they ever want to deal with the Parfitts again and, with respect, the feeling is entirely mutual.

I knew Rick was still with Marietta. And it still hurt.

Patty Parfitt

Sometimes I wondered if I'd done the right thing. Should I have let him have his cake and eat it as he'd wanted? No. I knew that he was itching to leave Marietta. He was reunited with Debbie Ash for a time behind Marietta's back but Debbie wasn't interested in taking Rick on full time it seemed — and who can blame her — so apparently Rick dumped her before she had the chance to enjoy doing it to him again.

I knew he was also playing around with an older, London society lady. She may not have been the best looker in the world — people said she looked like a witch — but she was a coke freak and was able to get Rick his supplies. Once again he had claimed publicly that he was Mr Squeaky Clean now he was back with Marietta, but that wasn't true. Marietta didn't know it but he was still drinking, doing coke occasionally, and he was back on the grass!

The rest of the band aren't exactly pure as driven snow either. I know Francis still smokes and he lets his children do drugs in the house. Simon and Keiron smoked dope at home and Nicholas took some acid once some time ago. It was four times the normal dose and it really did his head in. He was on a high for nearly two months and tried to kill himself. Francis used to phone him from touring and he would tell Francis that he was an alien because he knew what they looked like, that he was evil and every car numberplate began with the letter E. Eileen, Francis' wife, had a very difficult time with him when Francis was away.

Andy Bown also lets his son and daughter smoke at home. The children, he says, have seen it every day of their lives so it's natural to them.

Amazingly, the band all seem to be quite fit but I always thought it was all bound to catch up with Rick one day and it did in May 1997.

Rick was making a cup of tea at home in the Quay West flat. He'd already had some chest pains but, typically, ignored them. He works on the theory that if you ignore aches, pains or hangovers they go away — a bit like wives and girlfriends! The chest pain that day nearly knocked him over.

When it had lessened he called his doctor in Harley Street and went to see him the following afternoon at 3.00pm. By nine he was in hospital having a quadruple heart by-pass operation. He'd had a massive angina attack, all four arteries were closing up rapidly and he very nearly died.

I knew that physically Rick wasn't in great shape and God knows he's abused that poor old body for years and years. Even so, hearing that he was having heart surgery was a shock. Perhaps because the abuse has gone on so long we all thought he was indestructible — on tour they called him 'Rock'. I'm sure that's what he thought, too, so it must have been a terrible shock for him too.

We rang the hospital, just to find out how he was. No one had had the decency to ring and tell us, not even Lil. I didn't speak to Rick but Harry did.

There were even more shocks in store.

Marietta apparently rushed over from Germany to be with Rick in his hour of need but she was too late. She saw him and returned to Germany briefly, planning to fly back within days. What she didn't know was that Laura — Rick's long-lost friend from the old Marquee days — had popped her head round the corner of Quo's dressing room door when the band had played Wembley the Christmas before. They'd been having an affair ever since.

Poor Marietta. She was told that her presence was no longer required at the hospital bedside. 'I'll phone you later,' said Rick, 'I need time on my own.' Marietta found out about Laura a couple of days later when she read it in the *Sun*.

Rick and Laura revealed their undying love to the newspapers. And what a love story it was — almost identical to Rick and Marietta's and probably ours, too!

Patty Parfitt

Rick was asked by the reporters about Marietta. I bet he didn't like that and he obviously was a bit evasive. He did admit that he and Marietta probably wouldn't be in touch any more.

I must admit I felt sorry for Marietta.

In a way I feel sorry for Laura, too. There may be hard times ahead.

Ah, happy memories. Been there, done that — so has Marietta.

As far as I know Rick and Laura are still together. Maybe I'm wrong, maybe this really is true love, maybe Rick really is a changed man. Fat chance.

Rick came to Harry's ninth birthday party to help out which meant the world to Harry.

Three months after his operation Rick was back on stage, still rockin' and rollin' all over the world. I don't think he'll ever stop and, whatever I feel for him personally, I still think Quo are a great band.

People crack jokes about their songs being based on the same three chords, but get out there and watch them on stage — they never fail to bring the place alive.

Now it's the end of the chapter — a very strange feeling. Now I can begin to build a new life for myself — and for Harry. But I'm still finding it difficult. I'm at a loss what to do, although knowing me something will turn up.

Tragically, in April of this year my father passed away after a few years of poor health, due to heart problems. Harry was terribly upset, but he was very brave and took care of his Nanny very well.

Fortunately I still have friends. The Tarrants are good friends and Kevin and Sue Godley were furious with Rick for the way he treated me and Harry.

There are some other friends I'd like to catch up with. Cheryl Baker is one. When we were at Silverdale she was a

Laughing All Over The World

really good mate and she invited us to her wedding. She was marrying Steve, a lovely chap who is a session musician with Cliff Richard's band and wrote some songs with him. I was really looking forward to it but Rick had to play a gig in Ireland.

Of course, I still think about Rick. I haven't slept with any man since him or even been out with anyone. My friends think I'm completely mad and are forever trying to drag me off to meet possibles. I've even had a few nice offers. But I haven't felt ready for another relationship. I was hurt too badly. The thought of another relationship scares me, the thought of making love scares me. For six years I've been on my own. I'd probably be murder to live with now — I like to do things *my* way. Nobody can tell me to do anything any more, and I don't see that changing.

But I'm happy enough, happy with Harry, optimistic about the future. I've got happy memories of laughing all over the world with Rick and Quo — and crying with love and pain.

My past didn't turn out as I expected so who knows what the future holds. For once I can't answer that.

Epilogue

Francis Rossi
Still with Quo, still regards himself as number one — but no new solo projects have got off the ground.

Jean Rossi
Last heard of living in a mobile home, and very bitter about Francis. I wish her well.

John Coghlan
He's still with Gillie — I last saw him when he suddenly popped up on an afternoon TV quiz show. They still keep in touch with the Lancasters and seem very happy.

Alan Lancaster
He's still hurt about the way Rick and Francis treated him but he's doing very well in the Australian property market and producing other artists. Dayle is now very successful, too, running her own interior design company. They are both wonderful friends to me.

Patty Parfitt

Colin Johnson
CJ, as they always called him, spends his time between his homes in Maidenhead and Tortolla in the Virgin Islands. He's busy writing a book and his latest management project is the electric rock harmony band Radar for whom, of course, he predicts great things!

Ron Brown
Sadly Ron, our great friend, is terminally ill with heart disease. He's on oxygen and morphine. Claire looks after him and he tries to keep cheerful — he's still as supportive, at least to me, as he ever was.

David Walker
Still managing the band, probably still pissed off at losing the court case against me for Rick and probably still playing poker whenever he gets the chance.

Ian Jones
I heard he's managing a songwriter who wrote a song for Jimmy Nail.

Alan Crux
He's probably still nervous, still biting his nails and pulling his hair. Last heard of building — probably single-handed — a holiday complex in Tenerife.

Rhino
Still with the band, still with Kathy.

Jeff
Still with the band, still with Helen — and probably still carrying his umbrella. Jeff is famous for his umbrella.

Andrew
Still with Caroline and buying more real estate.

Marietta
She's still in Germany in the big house built to please Rick. She's probably still working for Daddy. She's supposed to be working on a book, too, which I look forward to reading!

Richard Parfitt Jr.
He's still being looked after financially by his father and now enjoys the familiar Quo lifestyle. He likes go-karting and has ambitions to be a Formula One driver. Rick is confident that he has recovered from the Crohns Disease which has plagued his life.

Harry Parfitt
Harry has moved to prep school and is full of energy. He enjoys chess, squash, judo, swimming and all sports — I fear he's going to be like Rick in that way. His latest passion is golf! He's also joined the Stagecoach Drama School and he's doing well — and he now has a much better relationship with his father, I'm pleased to say.

Patty Parfitt
Surviving!

Rick Parfitt
Still laughing all over the world!